The Precious Blood of Jesus

The Precious Blood of Jesus

Francis Wale Oke

eagle

Guildford, Surrey

British Library Cataloguing in Publication Data. A catalogue record for this book is available from the British Library.

Published by Eagle, an imprint of Inter Publishing Service (IPS) Ltd, PO Box 530, Guildford, Surrey GU2 5FH.

First published in Nigeria in 1985 by His Kingdom House, P.O.Box 2559, Plumstead, London SE 18 1ZB; and LIDATO Building 1, Subulade St, Off Liberty Rd, P.O. Box 36506, Dugbe, Ibadan Nigeria.

Scripture quotations, unless otherwise noted, are taken from the King James Version.

Typeset by Eagle
Printed by Cox & Wyman

ISBN No: 0 86347 321 0

DEDICATION

Affectionately dedicated to all the Elders, Pastors,
Deacons, Deaconnesses and every member of
Christ Life Church worldwide.

Words cannot adequately express
what you all mean to me.

Through the blood of the Lamb we shall continue
to move from victory to victory, from
exploits to exploits, from glory to glory
until we reach our eternal home.

And they overcame him by the blood of the Lamb,
and by the word of their testimony;
they loved not their lives unto the death.
Revelations 12:11

ACKNOWLEDGEMENTS

A successful, beautiful concert is the product of a dedicated team that has worked in harmony. This is the summary of what you now have in your hands. It is the product of the faithful labour of several dedicated people of God who really want the message of this book to come to you, to bless you. They are too numerous to mention by name, but I must acknowledge some here.

I hereby register my appreciation of, and gratitude to, these brethren that have been instrumental to the production of this work.

Pastor Remi Oyejide who was there the day 'we prayed through' on the revelation, Mrs Adejoke Oyejide who laboured to typeset the original script, Mrs Sue Wavre who edited it to suit our European and international readers, Mr David Wavre and the team at Eagle who worked so hard to beat that 'impossible' deadline, the entire staff of *The Sword of the Spirit Ministries* who are always there, and all my partners who by their prayers and support have kept this work going and growing.

Special thanks to Pastor and Mrs Runsewe whose financial support over the years have blessed this great work. And to my sweetheart, Victoria, who really is the choicest amongst all women.

God bless you all. Together we are stepping into our better days. You will grow stronger by the day. In Jesus' mighty name.

Francis Wale Oke
Ibedan, Nigeria

CONTENTS

Introduction

The Blood of Jesus

There is tremendous power in the blood of Jesus. Everyone ought to **know** what the blood of Jesus Christ stands for, **appreciate** it and **take advantage** of its power, thereby enjoying the **unlimited blessings** it carries for all mankind.

When Jesus shed His precious blood, He offered the only sacrifice needed to provide for all your needs in time and in eternity.

This precious blood **means everything before the throne of God.** It is the **only means** by which God can give you acceptance. It is the **only means** by which you can have access to God's presence and into all the blessings He has for you.

This precious blood means everything to Satan our adversary and all his hosts. They know it is by this blood they suffered everlasting defeat. They have no answer to the blood of Jesus. Absolutely none.

Your total victory in this world is in the blood of Jesus Christ. It is the means by which you can overcome the hostile forces of darkness that are set in array against you and be truly more than a conqueror.

God says, *'My people are destroyed for lack of knowledge'* (Hosea 4:6). When you know, understand and apply the vital truth that the Bible teaches about the blood of Jesus Christ, you will be completely free from sin, from fear, sicknesses, deception, curses and from every negative work of the devil. And you will walk in dominion over the earth. This is the will of God for you. *'And ye shall know the truth, and the truth shall make you free'* (John 8:32).

The blood of Jesus is the key to abundant life, forgiveness, peace, victory, deliverance, healing and hope. The full benefits of the **complete redemption** that Jesus Christ brought for all mankind is in His blood.

In order to fully experience the power of the blood of Jesus, you need to **know, believe, appropriate** and **expect** the blessings it carries.

Know: Know the truth about the life, and grace and power that is in the blood of Jesus. There is enough power in that blood to meet all of your needs.

Believe: Believe all that God's Word says about the blood of Jesus. It will be to you according to your faith.

Appropriate: Take personal advantage of the life, the power, that is in the blood of Jesus. It will not work for you until you personally appropriate it.

Expect: Expect your miracle, your victory, your breakthrough, your cleansing, as you take advantage of the blood. Expect God to confirm His Word in your life.

Equipped to Overcome

I first wrote a booklet on this subject in 1985. It was so well received that thousands of copies were sold within the first few months of its release. Then I had a specific leading of the Lord to completely re-write the book in 1996, based on deeper insight the Lord has given me into this all-important subject. In the first quarter of 1997, I was reviewing the material as I carried the file with me everywhere I went. It was so rich, so refreshing. It mightily blessed me.

Spiritual Warfare

Spiritual warfare is normal for God's champions. It is not new today, it began long, long ago. But we are destined to win. Take a look at this passage with me.

> *And there was war in heaven: Michael and his angels fought against the dragon; and the dragon fought and his angels, and prevailed not; neither was their place found any more in heaven. And the great dragon was cast out, that old serpent, called the Devil, and Satan, which deceiveth the whole world: he was cast out into the earth, and his angels were cast out with him. And I heard a loud voice saying in heaven, Now is come salvation, and strength, and the kingdom of our God, and the power of his Christ: for the accuser of our brethren is cast down, which accused them before our God day and night. And they overcame him by the blood of the Lamb, and by the word of their testimony; and they loved not their lives unto the death.*
>
> Revelation 12:7–11

'And there was war in heaven.' That is where it started.

'And the dragon fought and his angels.' Those are our principal enemies; not men, although they can be used. The enemy is the dragon.

'Michael and his angels fought.' You should not be afraid, for those that are with us are more than those that are against us (II Kings 6:16). In the battle of life you are not alone. For every angel of darkness that is against you, there are at least two mighty angels of light that are with you and for you. And the throne of

God is behind you to back you up. No matter the storms, your victory is certain if you put your faith in the blood of the Lamb.

Certain things happened to the dragon and his angels.

- The dragon did not, could not prevail.
- The dragon was cast out and his angels.
- Their place was no longer available. Their seats were removed. Their positions cancelled. They lost their standing outright.

This is what God wants to do in your life. No matter what you are going through; if you put your total trust in God and appropriate the power that is in the blood of Jesus Christ:

- The dragon cannot prevail.
- The dragon must be cast out.
- The stronghold of the enemy shall be wiped out.

God is set to do all these for you today. How did it happen then?

> *And they overcame him by the blood of the Lamb, and by the word of their testimony; and they loved not their lives unto the death.*
>
> Revelation 12:11

We can see three things that brought absolute victory.

- They overcome by the blood of the Lamb.
- They overcame by the word of their testimony.
- They overcame because they were totally sold out to God, not caring for their lives.

Victory is available to you today.

First, do not try to save your life. Give yourself

completely to God. Submit to His will. Humble yourself under His mighty hand. Let your obedience to Him be complete. And do exactly what He has told you to do. If you try to save your life you will lose it. If you yield your life fully to Him He will save you.

Secondly, take a hold on the blood of Jesus the Lamb of God. Having yielded yourself to God, the blood of Jesus becomes an 'atomic bomb' in your hands, as it were, to completely neutralise the position of the enemy. There is power in the blood of Jesus to give you victory today.

Thirdly, make your testimony bold. Make it loud. Make it clear. Your testimony of victory and grace is a weapon the enemy cannot withstand.

The testimony of your confidence in the blood of Jesus is a two-edged sword that will literally finish off the enemy. Be bold. Be strong. The Lord is with you like a mighty warrior if indeed you have yielded yourself to Him. Use your testimony boldly and put the enemy on the run.

In 1997, the enemy came against me like a devouring storm. It happened right in the midst of a great harvest of souls. We had just planted thirty churches in one month. We followed that with heavy crusades attracting several thousands. Then we hosted a Ministers' Conference where thousands of ministers were ignited to possess the gates of the enemy. The power of God flowed freely and those precious servants of God went wild for Jesus. Then we moved into a crusade where close to two hundred thousand gathered in one service to receive the Word of life. The enemy became really angry and wanted to crush us. But our house was built on God's eternal foundation.

The Word of God was our sure anchor, the mercies

of God our mainstay. The One inside us was the all-conquering One. He gave us peace in the midst of storms that came from all fronts. He gave us absolute victory over the adversary and moved us into a new dimension of His grace. To Him alone we give all the glory.

That is exactly what He wants to do for you – by the blood of the Lamb. Claim your complete victory today as you are obedient to the Word. You are more than a conqueror, through the blood of Jesus.

> *And they overcame him by the blood of the Lamb,*
> *and by the word of their testimony; and they loved*
> *not their lives unto the death.*
>
> Revelation 12:11

God is set to honour the blood of His Son Jesus in your life. Begin to take advantage of the blood of Jesus today. Take refuge in the blood of the everlasting covenant. Then you will begin to see the power of God at work in a whole new dimension in your life, as never before. The devil will be totally defeated and God will be glorified. Then Jesus will be satisfied that He has not shed His precious blood in vain on your behalf. He is pleased when you are taking maximum advantage of the blessings He has bought for you by His precious blood.

1

Jesus Christ:
The Hope of the World

The blood of Jesus is the only hope for all mankind. This is a sweeping statement but it is the truth. Without the blood of Jesus there is no hope of reconciliation with God. There is no hope of forgiveness or cleansing from sin. There is no hope of ever entering heaven or enjoying eternal glory. Thank God Jesus shed His precious blood. Now there is hope for every person on the face of the earth – through the precious blood of Jesus, the Lamb of God. No matter what your situation and circumstances, in the blood of Jesus Christ there is hope for you. This is the message God has given me for you, hold on to it and move today from your dungeon into the light of God's favour.

In 1987, while I was conducting a meeting in Lagos, a young lady came under such conviction of the Holy Spirit about her spiritual state that she became very depressed. After one afternoon session she came to speak with me. She had been a Muslim but was not serious about her religion. She had been living a very loose life, going out with several men, and she felt filthy. She thought God could never forgive her; she was in tears. I patiently took her through the Scriptures, pointing her to the precious blood of

Jesus, the Lamb of God.

At a certain point her face lit up, literally. 'Sir, you mean there is hope for me?' 'Yes,' I said, urging her to

No matter what your situation and circumstances, in the blood of Jesus Christ there is hope for you.

look away from herself, from her past, and look to the Lamb of God. And God helped her. She looked to Jesus and she was saved. During the evening meeting she was filled with the Holy Spirit. She is now married to a deacon in a Pentecostal church in Lagos and they are serving God happily together.

There is power in the blood of Jesus to transform the **vilest** sinner into a beautiful saint of the Most High God.

Blood Is Unique

Blood is a distinctly qualitative and incomparably valuable material in the spiritual realm. It cannot be manufactured in the scientist's laboratory, or created by man's ingenuity. It flows straight from God and carries the life of the flesh *'for the life of the flesh is in the blood'* (Leviticus 17:11). This is why people all over the world believe in the spiritual significance of blood.

From primitive time, man has recognized the spiritual value of blood and has tried to use it for religious purposes in one form or another. Even witches, wizards, familiar spirits and other agents of the devil understand the spiritual efficacy of blood, hence their insatiable appetite for it. But when it comes to taking away sin, bringing man into fellowship with God and obtaining absolute victory over the devil, the blood of goats and bulls can do nothing.

Neither can the blood of any human being. Thank God for the precious blood of Jesus, the only true remedy for man's spiritual problem.

The foundational problem of man is sin. Take sin away and he is completely all right. Before man fell in the Garden of Eden there was no problem at all. All the innumerable problems that have plagued man down the ages are the aftermath of sin and the fall. Hence, any seeming solution that does not address the fundamental issue of sin in man is only, at best, a cosmetic solution. Until sin is effectively dealt with, man is not free at all, no matter what he has or does.

And, indeed, unless blood is shed there can be neither pardon nor cleansing from sin. The Bible says,

> *And almost all things are by the law purged with blood; and without shedding of blood is no remission.*
>
> Hebrews 9:22

Sin Is Spiritual

Now, sin is a spiritual affair. When you sin against God you break His spiritual law and create an imbalance, a disorder in His universe. This imbalance must be balanced . . . must be compensated for . . . must be fully paid for. The righteousness and justice of God demand it! And righteousness and truth are the foundations of God's throne. He ceases to be God when He ceases to be altogether just and righteous. Every sin must be judged and justly punished.

Charles G. Finney, the nineteenth-century American evangelist had this to say about the issue:

> Sin is the most expensive thing in the universe. Nothing else can cost so much. Pardoned or

unpardoned, its cost is infinitely great.
Pardoned, the cost falls chiefly on the great
atoning substitute; unpardoned, it must fall on
the head of the sinner.

When you sin it has to be atoned for, otherwise you
die spiritually. The Bible is very clear on this: *'The soul
that sinneth, it shall die . . .'* (Ezekiel 18:20a), because
'the wages of sin is death' (Romans 6:23).

Just one sin is sufficient to defile and render you
unclean in the sight of the Lord God of all the earth,
who is absolutely holy. You do not need to commit
many sins to become unclean and unworthy.

How many sins did Adam
and Eve commit before they
were driven from the presence
of God? Just one. One sin is sufficient to banish you forever
from His presence. This is God's
standard of holiness. After
Adam and Eve sinned, they
became guilty, defiled and were
separated from God. They actu-
ally died spiritually, for death literally means 'separation'. Be-cause *'the wages of sin is death'*, they paid the
first penalty due for their disobedience and rebelliousness.

*The precious blood
of Jesus, the only
true remedy for
man's spiritual
problem.*

Before God drove them out of His presence, He
killed an animal, spilled the blood and used the skin
to cover their nakedness, now exposed by sin. They
were not naked before the fall; they were covered by
the glory of God. Please understand that sin and the
glory of God cannot co-exist. As sin entered their
lives, the glory departed and they became naked and
exposed.

With the shedding of the blood of that animal, God instituted atonement for sin – a pointer to the time when the perfect substitute, Jesus, would come to bear the sin of the entire human race.

Sin is an awful reality in our world. It has tainted so many once-beautiful lives. It has destroyed so many precious souls who were originally made in God's image of splendour. It has ruined so many lives that held out such great hopes of a grand tomorrow. Every single soul burning in hell now is a victim of the awful reality of sin.

But there is a glorious reality that effectively deals with sin in man, no matter its shade or form – the precious blood of Jesus. This was exactly the message God was getting across in the Garden of Eden. In spite of His great love for man, He had to drive them out of His presence because of sin.

Yet even while banishing man, He held out hope. 'My Son is coming to shed his blood for you. His blood will deal with your sin in all its ramifications. By His blood the power of sin over your life shall be broken and destroyed and you will truly be what I want you to be.' This was what God was saying when he killed that animal in the garden, shed its blood and used its skin to cover the nakedness and shame of Adam and Eve.

Jesus has come, shed His blood and made grace available for you and me. This is the glorious reality that can supersede and invalidate the reality of sin if only you will believe and take advantage of it. Because the blood of Jesus has been shed for you, you can be cleansed from sin and be free from its awful grip and power for ever. There is power in the blood of Jesus to cleanse, to deliver, to set free and to make you as pure as God wants you to be.

The Story of Two Pastors

Let me tell you the actual stories of two pastors and how the blood of Jesus made a difference in their lives.

Let me call the first one Stephen (not his real name). A report came to me that Pastor Stephen stole money from the church's offering. I invited him to see me for a chat. By the time he came, he was already a vegetable – so broken, so sorrowful, so humbled. He acknowledged his sin and wept in repentance. I did not need to be hard on him. *'A bruised reed shall he not break, and the smoking flax shall he not quench: he shall bring forth judgment unto truth'* (Isaiah 42:3). I led him to repent and asked him to stay off the pulpit for some time to seek the face of the Lord and put his spiritual life in order. After a short while he was restored back to his job and he went steadily forward in the work of the ministry. His church started to grow. His members started to really bless him, because God was blessing him. Seven years later, he is one of the most fruitful pastors in the area and God blessed him a few weeks ago with a new car. Each time I see him I remember how powerful the blood of Jesus is in removing the ugly stain of sin.

Then there was the case of Pastor James (again not his real name). He was caught stealing the offering. He was reported to me and I called him to discuss the matter with a view of leading him to repentance. He denied vehemently that he had ever done this.

I counselled him that I was not a policeman investigating a crime but his helper to point him to the Lamb. God is gracious. He will forgive every sin that is genuinely repented of and brought to the blood of Jesus, except blasphemy against the Holy Spirit.

However, God cannot forgive a sin until it is truly repented of. As I was talking with Pastor James, I knew deep within me he was lying, but I let him off. Soon he resigned from our ministry to start his own church. Seven years later, a broken, shattered Pastor James came to my house in tears asking me to help him and saying that the matter we had discussed was true.

He no longer enjoyed the unction of the Holy Spirit. His life had degenerated. His congregation had dwindled to just seven people. He was so impoverished he needed help badly. While praying, the Holy Spirit told him to come and meet with me to sort out his life. He did not need to go through all this suffering. If, like Pastor Stephen, he had genuinely repented and taken advantage of the blood of the Lamb, he would have been cleansed and blessed.

It was in dying He gave us life. It was through death He vanquished the one who had the power of death, that is the devil. The Lamb of God has shed His blood. Complete redemption is available for us.

The Bible is very clear on this *'He that covereth his sins shall not prosper: but whoso confesseth and forsaketh them shall have mercy'* (Proverbs 28:13). When you cover your sins, blessings shall be far away. When you truly repent, mercies are available from the throne of grace – by the blood of the Lamb.

Be open before God. Let the blood of Jesus deal with the real issue of your life.

Life for Life

In the spiritual realm, it is life for life. Hence, for your sin to be forgiven and for you to live again, a life must be sacrificed for it . . . blood must flow.

However, goats, bulls and sheep are not valuable enough, so their blood cannot fully pay for your sin and blot it out. Only if you were a goat, a bull or a sheep would it have been sufficient. That is why Adam and Eve were still driven from the presence of God in spite of the blood of an animal that had been shed for them. The blood of that animal only **covered** their sin from the sight of a holy God. It had no power to **blot out** or **cancel** their sin. The sin still remained; it was only covered. The blood of animals does not have the power to cancel the sin of human beings.

No other human being can pay for your sin either, because by being a sinner himself he is not qualified. He too needs somebody to pay for his sins. *'For all have sinned, and come short of the glory of God'* (Romans 3:23).

God then had to do something. He desperately wanted to save man and restore him to full fellowship. But this cannot be until man's sin is taken out of the way absolutely. God will not fellowship with sin in any shade or form.

Sin can be taken away only by blood, for *'without the shedding of blood is no remission'* (Hebrews 9:22). Since no animal blood can take away man's sin and no other human blood can take away man's sin, God, because of His great love for man, had to do something to make salvation possible and available.

That was why God sent His only begotten Son Jesus, holy, sinless and without blemish, to become man's substitute by shedding His precious blood. This is made clear in several scriptures in the New Testament. First, God gave a promise of redemption immediately man fell, when he spoke these words of judgment to the serpent.

> 'And I will put enmity between thee and the woman, and between thy seed and her seed; it shall bruise thy head, and thou shalt bruise his heel.'
>
> Genesis 3:15

Jesus came into the world as the seed of the woman, not partaking of the seed of Adam that had been contaminated by sin. He was conceived of the Holy Ghost in the womb of the virgin Mary. When He died on the cross of Calvary, He executed judgment on the serpent by smashing his head forever.

When Jesus died and His blood was shed, He did what goats, bulls, sheep or any human being could not do. Not only did He defeat the devil once and for all, he also made a perfect sacrifice for our sins. This sacrifice was perfectly acceptable to God. This is why we can receive perfect salvation – because Jesus has shed His precious blood.

> For it is not possible that the blood of bulls and of goats should take away sins . . . but this man [Jesus], after he had offered one sacrifice for sins for ever, sat down on the right hand of God; from henceforth expecting till his enemies be made his footstool. **For by one offering he hath perfected for ever them that are sanctified.**
>
> Hebrews 10:4, 12–14 (my emphasis)

Jesus really needed to die. Not for Himself, but because of us. Otherwise we are without hope. He did not die in vain. He knew no sin, but God made Him to be sin for us. By deliberately laying down His life for us out of His great love, we can have forgiveness and the remission of our sins, and enter into intimate fellowship with God once again.

The blood is still living and flowing, and it cleanses from *'all sin'* (I John 1:7).

> *But if we walk in the light, as he is in the light, we*
> *have fellowship one with another, and the blood of*
> *Jesus Christ his Son cleanseth us from **all sin***.
>
> I John 1:7 (my emphasis)

No matter who you are or what your case may be, you can take advantage of that blood right away and be washed from your sins. If really you are interested in salvation from sin, if really you want true redemption, if really you want peace with God, this is your only hope – the blood of Jesus.

> *Neither is there salvation in any other: for there is*
> *none other name under heaven given among men,*
> *whereby we must be saved.*
>
> Acts 4:12

The Great Revelation

God showed John, the beloved, an awesome scene in heaven. Here is a book, completely sealed, inside and outside, held in the hand of the One sitting upon the throne – the Most High God. This book contains the details of God's plan for the redemption of all mankind. Unless it is opened there is no hope for any single person in the human race. Adam had sold us to the devil through disobedience a long while ago and so we are in slavery. But here is God's plan of full salvation and complete redemption – who would unfold it?

The search commenced.

In the whole of heaven, among the ranks of the angelic hosts and heavenly beings, not one qualified. Not even an archangel. They do not know of the glory and wonder of the redemption story. These are *'things the angels desire to look into'* (I Peter 1:12). They are not qualified even to tell the story.

> *Look away from yourself, otherwise all you see is your sinfulness . . . Look to Jesus the Lamb of God and you will never be the same again.*

On earth below the search went on. Among the ranks of men no single person qualified . . . not any of the great prophets or religious leaders or priests or imams or kings or princes or queens or governors or gurus or sheiks. They too were all waiting for a redeemer.

Beneath the earth they are not qualified to even look into the face of Him who sits upon the throne, certainly not to take the book from His hand.

Does that mean there is no hope for mankind? John broke down in tears:

> *And no man in heaven, nor in earth, neither under the earth, was able to open the book, neither to look thereon. And I wept much, because no man was found worthy to open and to read the book, neither to look thereon.*

Revelation 5:3–4

It was then that one of the elders before the throne of God spoke a word of comfort to John. All is not lost. Although none other was found worthy, there is One who qualified. There is One who prevailed, there is One who did it, Jesus Christ the Lamb of God. He gave His life, He shed His blood, He prevailed against the adversaries, He finished the job.

> *And one of the elders saith unto me, Weep not: behold, the Lion of the tribe of Juda, the Root of David, hath prevailed to open the book, and to loose the seven seals thereof. And I beheld, and, lo, in the midst of the throne and of the four beasts, and in the midst of the elders, stood a Lamb as it had been slain, having seven horns and seven eyes, which are the seven Spirits of God sent forth into all the earth. And he came and took the book out of the right hand of him that sat upon the throne.*
>
> Revelation 5:5–7

There should be no doubt in your mind, Jesus Christ is the Redeemer of all mankind, the only hope of the world, who has revealed God's plan of salvation and made it possible for us to be cleansed from our sin and to enter into God's presence.

How did He do it? He prevailed as the slain Lamb of God. It was in dying He gave us life. It is through death He vanquished the one who had the power of death, that is, the devil. The Lamb of God has shed His blood. Complete redemption is available for us.

The blood was shed for you to redeem you from sin and all the curses of the law and to restore all that the first Adam lost, and much more. It is of Christ that this is written:

> *Look unto me, and be ye saved, all the ends of the earth: for I am God, and there is none else.*
>
> Isaiah 45:22

You do not need to do very much in order to enjoy full salvation. Jesus Christ has purchased complete redemption for us with His precious blood. Just look to Him and be saved, healed, delivered, preserved and protected – for time and eternity. Look away from yourself, otherwise all you see is your sinfulness. Look away from men, where you have met with so much disappointment. Look away from your idols, your pets, your props upon which you have leaned for so long in vain. Look to Jesus the Lamb of God and you will never be the same again.

2

Behold the Lamb of God

When John the Baptist saw Jesus Christ, he proclaimed:

Behold the Lamb of God, which taketh away the sin of the world.

John 1:29b

Jesus Christ is the Lamb of God that was slain for us. By His blood He brought us life, forgiveness, peace and joy. He brought us healing and health, deliverance and liberty. By His blood He delivered us from the wrath to come, purifying our consciences from filthiness, to serve the living God. He has made a way for us to enter into God's presence and call Him Father. Heaven is a glorious reality; only by the blood of the Lamb.

Do not mistake me. The blood of Jesus is not an excuse for allowing sin in your life. No, never. Rather, the blood of Jesus is God's effective solution to the problem of sin. It delivers from sin and keeps us pure and free as we walk in the light. The blood of Jesus is God's remedy for the sin problem.

God is fully satisfied with the sacrifice of the blood of His Son. There is nothing more to add. When we plead that blood in faith, God honours our plea promptly. Speaking prophetically about the blood of Jesus, Zechariah said this under the anointing of the Holy Spirit:

As for thee also, by the blood of thy covenant I have sent forth thy prisoners out of the pit wherein is no water. Turn you to the strong hold, ye prisoners of hope: even to day do I declare that I will render double unto thee.

Zechariah 9:11–12

When I was about nine years old, I had an experience that graphically illustrates what it means to be in a pit 'wherein is no water'. I spent the first eleven years of my life in a village in the south-western part of Nigeria. During the dry season, water was always a rare commodity; we would go around searching for it. One day, when out looking, we got to a place where there was a little water in a pit, but we had to wade through a large pool of mud before getting to the water. I managed to struggle through and filled my bucket. Carrying the bucket on my head, I tried to cross the pond back to dry land; but I got stuck – right in the miry clay where there was no water. I struggled hard to be free, but the harder I struggled the deeper I sank. I was trapped in a pit 'wherein was no water'! I had to shout for help until a stronger and more mature person came to pull me out.

Your pit 'wherein [is] no water' may be a particular sin or sinful habit. It may be some demonic bondage. It may be the spirit of fear. It may be an addiction to lust and immoral thoughts. It may be the horrible nightmares you experience from time to time. It may be severe depression and the spirit of heaviness. It may be oppressive poverty and a failure syndrome. Whatever holds you down and keeps you bound, is *'a pit wherein is no water'*.

Man is a prisoner of hope, right inside that pit. He is forever hoping for freedom, forever searching for deliverance, forever fighting for liberation. The blood of Jesus Christ is the Stronghold, the Liberation, the Ransom you have long been searching for. His blood has brought victory for us. You can now turn to your Stronghold by faith and claim complete liberty as you take advantage of this precious blood.

God has ordained the blood of Jesus for your freedom. Turn to the blood of Jesus today, and be free from your pit. No matter what that pit is, it cannot withstand the blood. There is power in the blood of Jesus to break and destroy every stronghold.

The blood has delivered and set me free. The blood still covers me right now. My faith for victory is in the blood of Jesus. I have no other ground on which to stand. The blood of Jesus is sufficient for me.

I have seen people experience complete forgiveness, total cleansing and victory by putting their faith in the blood of Jesus. You can enjoy the same as you act out your faith. The blood of Jesus is God's provision for your complete redemption.

In whom [Jesus] we have redemption through his blood, even the forgiveness of sins.
Colossians.1:14

Complete redemption is available for you today by the blood of the Lamb. You can be forgiv-

> **The blood of Jesus Christ is the Stronghold, the Liberation, the Ransom you have long been searching for. His blood has brought victory for us. You can now turn to your Stronghold by faith and claim complete liberty as you take advantage of this precious blood.**

en all your sins right now. You can enjoy peace with
God. You can be free from all that the devil has bound
you with. You can be free indeed . . . Right now. Then
you will be able to sing with David a song of deliverance and victory.

I waited patiently for the LORD;
And he inclined unto me, and heard my cry.
He brought me up also out of an horrible pit,
  out of the miry clay,
And set my feet upon a rock, and established
  my goings.
And he hath put a new song in my mouth,
  even praise unto our God:
Many shall see it, and fear,
And shall trust in the LORD.
                          Psalm 40:1–3 (my emphasis)

Behold the Lamb . . .

This statement of John the Baptist is God's heart-cry
to all mankind today. It is God's heart-cry to you. No
matter who you are, no matter what your situation is;
behold the Lamb of God!

There are two crucial applications of this scripture
that I want to explain here.

In the first instance it was uttered by John the
Baptist the first time he presented Jesus to the people
as the Messiah – the Anointed One – the long-expect-
ed Redeemer.

The next day John seeth Jesus coming unto him,
    and saith, ***Behold the Lamb of God, which***
taketh away the sin of the world.
                          John 1:29 (my emphasis)

For anyone to be free from sin and experience forgiveness and acceptance with God, he has to behold the Lamb of God who is the only One that can take away the sin of the world. This fulfils the prophecy of Isaiah, uttered almost eight hundred years before Christ was born:

> The blood has delivered and set me free. The blood still covers me right now.
> My faith for victory is in the blood of Jesus. I have no other ground on which to stand. The blood of Jesus is sufficient for me.

Turn to me and be saved,
  all you ends of the earth;
  for I am God, and there is no
    other.

Isaiah 45:22 (NIV)

It must be made clear that God has no alternative plan to save mankind. Jesus Christ is the only One God has ordained to carry your sins away. He did that through His precious blood.

> *Neither is there salvation in any other: for there is none other name under heaven given among men, whereby we must be saved.*
>
> Acts 4:12

Today, if anyone will sincerely look to the Lamb of God in faith, he will truly be saved – for time and eternity.

The second instance when John uttered this statement, *'Behold the Lamb . . .'*, the setting was quite different. Jesus had already been presented to the people as the Lamb of God that takes away the sins of the world. Many of them even believed in Him already because of John's testimony. So now Jesus is being presented as the Lamb of God to a people whose sins have been taken away because they already trust in Him.

Nevertheless they still needed to look to the Lamb and keep looking to Him in order **to be sustained in the grace of God.**

And looking upon Jesus as he walked, he saith, Behold the Lamb of God!

John 1:36

We need to behold the Lamb, not just for forgiveness, but also for grace and strength to run the race set before us; for victory and for exploits. If we are going to be sustained and upheld we need to keep looking to the Lamb. If we are to remain victorious and happy, we need to look to the Lamb. We must never at any point stop looking to the Lamb of God. He is our peace. He is our strength. He is our all in all. Like David, we are to set Him always before us and let Him be at our right hand. And we shall never be moved.

I have set the LORD always before me:
Because he is at my right hand, I shall not be moved.

Psalm 16:8

We are to run with patience the race that is set before us, *'looking unto Jesus, the author and finisher of our faith'* (Hebrews 12:2). This is the secret of unfailing strength.

Wherefore seeing we also are compassed about with so great a cloud of witnesses, let us lay aside every weight, and the sin which doth so easily beset us, and let us run with patience the race that is set

*before us, looking unto Jesus the author and finisher
of our faith; who for the joy that was set before him
endured the cross, despising the shame, and is set
down at the right hand of the throne of God.*

Hebrews 12:1–2

Beloved, the precious blood of Jesus was shed for
you, not only to give you forgiveness of sin, but also to give you absolute victory.

> *We must never
> look away
> from Him to our
> own strength or
> wisdom or
> riches or might.
> We are to trust
> in the Lord with
> all our heart.
> We are not to
> lean on our own
> understanding. We
> are to acknowledge
> God in all our
> ways and not lean
> on the arms of
> the flesh.*

Therefore, today, behold the Lamb of God!

We must never look away from Him to our own strength or wisdom or riches or might. We are to trust in the Lord with all our heart. We are not to lean on our own understanding. We are to acknowledge God in all our ways and not lean on the arms of the flesh.

Having begun the Christian race in the Spirit, we must not hope to be made perfect in the flesh. Our focus must forever be upon the Lamb, not on a man or some device or some strategy. Peter succeeded in walking on water as long as he kept looking to the Lamb. The moment he took his eyes off the Lamb he started to sink. It does not really matter how long you have walked with the Lord, if you take your eyes off Him you will begin to sink. And perhaps you are sinking already – into lukewarmness, into heresies and religious fads, into fear, apathy, sin, debt, oppression or depression. Lift up your eyes in faith. Look now to the Lamb of God and He will lift you up.

They looked unto him, and were lightened:
And their faces were not ashamed.

Psalm 34:5

3

The Precious Blood of Jesus

The blood of Jesus is very precious. We read in the Bible:

> *Forasmuch as ye know that ye were not redeemed with corruptible things, as silver and gold, from your vain conversation received by tradition from your fathers; but with the precious blood of Christ, as of a lamb without blemish and without spot.*

> I Peter 1:18–19

We understand from this scripture that the blood of Jesus is invaluably precious. It cannot be compared with silver or gold.

Why is it so precious? Here are a few reasons; I believe the Spirit of God will expound and illuminate the message.

It Redeems

It is the blood of Jesus that redeemed us; not only from the hands of the devil, but also from the curse of the law.

We were sold to Satan; we were under his dominion and oppression. The powers of darkness were having a field day with us and we could not help ourselves. But Jesus came and paid the price – not with silver or gold or any such material thing. All the silver and gold in the world put together cannot redeem

a single soul. But Jesus shed His precious blood and
that settled the bill.

Now the price is paid. It is finished. The dominion
of the devil and his hosts: finished. The oppression of
the powers of darkness: finished. We can now enjoy
full liberty because of the blood that was shed for us.
We can now give thanks to God our Father who has
made us partakers of His inheritance and has delivered us from the powers of darkness.

> *Giving thanks unto the Father, which hath made us*
> *meet to be partakers of the inheritance of the saints*
> *in light: who hath delivered us from the power of*
> *darkness, and hath translated us into the kingdom of*
> *his dear Son: in whom we have*
> *redemption through his blood,*
> *even the forgiveness of sins.*
>   Colossians 1:12–14

Everyone who has truly
believed in Christ and is fully
trusting in His blood can now
boldly claim total liberty from
every oppression of Satan and
the powers of darkness. You are
no more a slave to Satan. Jesus
has set you free for ever. *'If the
Son therefore shall make you free,
ye shall be free indeed'* (John 8:36).
You have been bought with a
price.

I read this illustration in one
of Dr Reuben Torrey's books. A
little boy once caught a spar-
row. The bird was trembling in his hand, struggling

*Now the price
is paid. It is
finished. The
dominion of the
devil and his hosts:
finished. The
oppression of
the powers of
darkness: finished.
We can now enjoy
full liberty because
of the blood that
was shed for us.*

to escape but it could not. Then a man, seeing the poor little bird, begged the boy to let it go as the bird could not do him any good.

The boy refused, he had chased it for three hours before he was able to catch it. Then the man offered to buy the bird. The boy agreed to a price and it was paid. The man then took the poor bird and held it out in his hand. It flew away rejoicing in its liberty. It was redeemed by the man.

Likewise, Jesus Christ redeemed us from Satan who was holding us captive. But it was not money He paid: He redeemed us by His blood. Now we are free. Glory be to God!

Looking at this scripture you will see that God puts our redemption in the past tense: *'Who hath delivered us from the power of darkness, and hath translated us into the kingdom of his dear Son'* (Colossians 1:13).

Please notice three crucial points about this scripture:

First, **you have been delivered already** from the powers of darkness. It does not say you will be delivered from the powers of darkness some day. If you have put your trust in the precious blood of Jesus, you have been delivered. The powers of darkness no longer have any claim over you. The blood of Jesus has broken and destroyed their chains. You now belong to Christ.

Secondly, **you have been translated into the kingdom of God's dear Son.** You are now in the kingdom of Jesus, the kingdom of light. He is your Lord. Your Saviour. Your Master. Your King. Christ now rules over you in love and righteousness. Satan can no longer dominate or oppress your life. The blood of Jesus has freed you forever.

Thirdly, **Satan has no authority over you whatsoever.** You are no longer in his kingdom. He has no rule, no control, no say over the affairs of your life. None at all. Let me illustrate this. In the early eighties, Nigeria's political set-up collapsed as the military sacked the government of the day and seized rulership. Many of the politicians were clamped into jail without any formal charge whatsoever. They were accused of gross corruption, embezzlement and mismanagement. A good number of them managed to escape to Britain where they were granted political asylum. Because they were now in another kingdom, Nigeria's military government's laws no longer applied to them. Representations were made to the government of the United Kingdom for the extradition of these politicians, but the British government firmly but politely declined. The politicians were in another kingdom altogether. Hence, they were spared the shame, humiliation, torture and untimely deaths visited upon a good number of their colleagues.

What am I saying? You are now in another kingdom. You are no more under the influence of the devil. You are delivered from all satanic oppression and torment. Only through the precious blood of Christ.

When Jesus hung on the cross where His blood was drained, He bore all our sins on His body.

He literally became a curse for us, because it was people that were cursed that died that way.

Why did He choose to bear such a great shame? To redeem us from the curse of the law and set us free from its demands. This is made clear in the Bible:

Christ hath redeemed us from the curse of the law,

being made a curse for us: for it is written, Cursed is every one that hangeth on a tree: that the blessing of Abraham might come on the Gentiles through Jesus Christ; that we might receive the promise of the Spirit through faith.

Galatians 3:13–14

The blood also redeemed us from the curse of the law. The law condemned us, but Christ has satisfied the claims of the law. He tasted death for every man and made it possible for us to be saved.

. . . blotting out the handwriting of ordinances that was against us, which was contrary to us, and took it out of the way, nailing it to his cross.

Colossians 2:14

Now that I have trusted Christ and His blood, there is no more condemnation for me. What the law could not do Christ has done. I am saved by His blood. I am redeemed from the curse. Glory to God.

It Blots out Our Sins

It is the blood of Jesus Christ that blots out the sins of all who believe in Him. This is something to really praise God for. The very moment you believe Christ as your Saviour and Lord your sins are washed away completely.

The blood purges our conscience from all filthiness and makes it really pure so we can serve the Lord. The Bible says:

For if the blood of bulls and of goats, and the ashes of an heifer sprinkling the unclean, sanctifieth to the purifying of flesh: how much more shall the blood of Christ, who through the eternal Spirit offered him-

*self without spot to God, purge your conscience
from dead works to serve the living God?*
Hebrews 9:13–14

I have seen drunkards, harlots, armed robbers and
wicked liars washed in this precious blood, now having a pure conscience and a brand new life, serving
the Lord with joy and great excitement. The marvel of
it all is that when these sins are blotted out they will
never again be remembered against you. This is part
of the terms of the new covenant. God says:

> *For this is the covenant that I will make with the
>   house of Israel
> After those days, saith the Lord;
> I will put my laws into their mind,
> And write them in their hearts:
> And I will be to them a God,
> And they shall be to me a people . . .
> For I will be merciful to their unrighteousness,
> And their sins and their iniquities will I remember
>   no more.*

Hebrews 8:10, 12

David, having experienced this cleansing by faith,
declared:

> *He hath not dealt with us after our sins;
> Nor rewarded us according to our iniquities.
> For as the heaven is high above the earth,
> So great is his mercy toward them that fear him.
> **As far as the east is from the west,
> So far hath he removed our transgressions from
>   us.***

Psalm 103:10–12 (my emphasis)

How far is the east from the west? So far has the blood of Jesus removed those sins from you if you have truly trusted him. East and West can meet at a round-table conference politically, but in geography you can never bring the east and west together. The harder you try, the more impossible it becomes. They are infinitely separated. Can you see what the blood of Jesus has done to your sins? God has removed your sins from you as far as the east is from the west, because you have trusted in the blood of the Lamb. If you have not yet trusted Him for forgiveness you can trust Him today and experience the cleansing that is in His blood.

In the Old Testament, **'atone'** is the word commonly used in connection with the blood of animals shed for sacrifices. To atone means to cover. The blood of the animals merely covered sins. The people were still under the power of these sins. Not once in the New Testament is the word 'atone' used in connection with the blood of Jesus. In Romans 5:11 where the King James version used 'atonement' it is 'reconciliation' in the NIV. Several other translators agree with this.

> *I have seen drunkards, harlots, armed robbers and wicked liars washed in this precious blood, now having a pure conscience and a brand new life, serving the Lord with joy and great excitement.*

Why is the word 'atonement' not used in connection with the blood of Jesus? It is because atonement in the Old Testament was only a shadow of the real thing to come. The blood of Jesus

Christ does not just 'atone' or cover sins, it remits, purges or blots them out completely, doing such a perfect job of it that we are not only free from the guilt but also from the tyranny of sin. That is why it is possible for a Christian to live a holy life – through the precious blood of Jesus Christ.

It Brings Us into Fellowship with God

The blood of Jesus Christ brings us into close fellowship with God Almighty.

God is holy. He has nothing to do with sin.

Being so sinful we were separated from Him. The Bible even says we *'were without Christ, being aliens from the commonwealth of Israel, and strangers from the covenants of promise, having no hope, and without God in the world:'* (Ephesians 2:12).

Without hope! Without God! It was as bad as that.

But now in Christ Jesus ye who sometimes were far off are made nigh by the blood of Christ.

Ephesians 2:13

The blood has closed the gap between God and us. We can now enter into intimate fellowship with the Almighty.

In Old Testament times, only the high priest could enter into the most holy place, the holy of holies, where the Shekinah glory of God was; and that only once in a year. In order to do this he had to be totally covered with blood – the blood of animals. Otherwise he could not go near the holy of holies; he would have been struck dead at once.

But when Jesus died and shed His blood, He opened the way into the holy of holies. The Bible says that when He died, the curtain of the temple was rent in two, thus indicating that, by His death, the way is now open for us into the very presence of God Almighty. Right now anybody who trusts in the blood of Jesus can approach God any time, any day. Jesus our High Priest has opened the way for us through His precious blood. We now have boldness to enter into the holy of holies by the blood of Jesus.

> *God has removed your sins from you as far as the east is from the west, because you have trusted in the blood of the Lamb.*

We can share intimate fellowship with God. We can hear Him speak to us clearly and distinctly. We can also open our hearts to Him in prayer and get results. This would have been utterly impossible were it not for the blood of Jesus that was shed to close the gulf between God and man.

This is why any time I go into the presence of the Lord to pray, I start out by pleading the blood of Jesus upon myself. I know the Father is pleased when He sees me covered in the blood of Jesus. I am accepted in the Beloved so I can have sweet communion with my Daddy.

Having therefore, brethren, boldness to enter into the holiest by the blood of Jesus, by a new and living way, which he hath consecrated for us, through the veil, that is to say, his flesh; and having an high priest over the house of God; let us draw near with a true heart in full assurance of faith, having our hearts sprinkled from an evil conscience, and our bodies washed with pure water. Let us hold fast the profession of our faith without wavering; (for he is faithful that promises).

Hebrews 10:19–23

It Makes Peace

Peace is a scarce commodity in our world today. There are peace movements and peace talks all over the world, but it is the blood of Jesus Christ alone that makes peace.

And having made peace through the blood of his cross.

Colossians 1:20

When Jesus Christ shed His blood on the cross of Calvary He made peace available for all who trust Him.

No one can truly have peace of mind and a clear conscience without trusting in the blood of Jesus. No one can have peace with God outside the blood of Jesus. But when the blood of Jesus is sincerely applied there is peace indeed. He is the Prince of Peace. When He was leaving earth Jesus said to His disciples:

Peace I leave with you, my peace I give unto you: not as the world giveth, give I unto you. Let not your heart be troubled, neither let it be afraid.

John 14:27

This is an invaluable legacy. Through the blood of Jesus we have perfect peace that nothing can disturb in this trouble-ridden world.

Do you really want peace of heart? Do you want to be free from fears and the troubles of this present age? Just trust in the blood of Jesus. He says *'Come unto me, all ye that labour and are heavy laden, and I will give you rest'* (Matthew 11:28).

All your labours, conflicts and struggles cease when you lay your burdens on Jesus Christ and are washed by faith in His blood. Then He will keep you in perfect peace.

> *Thou wilt keep him in perfect peace, whose mind is stayed on thee: because he trusteth in thee.*
>
> Isaiah 26:3

Let your heart rest in Him by faith. Your peace is guaranteed one hundred per cent.

It Justifies

It is the blood of Jesus Christ that justifies. Everyone who has been born again needs to know that he has been justified. You need to know that nobody can lay anything against you before God; that there is no more condemnation for you. You have passed from death to life. You are justified.

When you say a man is justified, using our legal terminology today you mean he is **discharged and acquitted.** He has no case to answer. He has a clear record. This is what the blood of Jesus does for us. It blots out all our filthy past and gives us a new standing before God. I am so glad God has nothing against me anymore. I am His. He has justified me by the blood of Jesus.

No one can truly have peace of mind and a clear conscience without trusting in the blood of Jesus.

But God commendeth his love toward us, in that, while we were yet sinners, Christ died for us. Much more then, being now justified by his blood, we shall be saved from wrath through him.

Romans 5:8–9

There is therefore now no condemnation to them which are in Christ Jesus, who walk not after the flesh, but after the Spirit.

Romans 8:1

Do you now know you are justified by the blood of Jesus? In spite of all the devil is trying to do you have no case to answer. You are 'ransomed, healed, restored, forgiven'. You are justified freely by His grace through the blood that He shed for you. You are to stand fast in this knowledge and rejoice in what God has done for you.

The Blood Cleanses

There is cleansing power in the blood of Jesus. It is the only thing that can totally cleanse from sin.

When David sinned against God he was brokenhearted. Repenting, he pleaded: *'Wash me throughly from mine iniquity, and cleanse me from my sin'* (Psalm 51:2). Sin is a plague. You need to be thoroughly washed and totally cleansed from it, otherwise it defiles, weakens and destroys. But thanks be to God for the blood of Jesus Christ which cleanses from all sins.

But if we walk in the light, as he is in the light, we have fellowship one with another, and the blood of Jesus Christ his Son cleanseth us from all sin.

I John 1:7

This brings us to the question: What happens if a believer sins? Although this is discussed fully in a later chapter, let us mention here something about it in relation to the cleansing power of the blood of Jesus.

It is good to know that it is not the nature of true believers, who have been really born again, to make a habit of sinning. Sin becomes distasteful and repulsive to you the moment you are born again. Also, it is not the Father's will and pleasure that a believer should sin at all. This is why He has given us His Word, so that by meditating on it and keeping it in our heart we may be sanctified and kept from sinning.

> *Thy word have I hid in mine heart,*
> *That I may not sin against thee.*
>   Psalm 119:11

Again He says:

> *My little children, these things write I unto you,*
> *that ye sin not.*
>   I John 2:1

But if it happens that a believer falls into sin, the battle is not lost at all. God has made adequate provision for forgiveness and cleansing and restoration, if that believer is truly sorry and repents of the sin.

Remember, anyone that covers up his sins shall not prosper; but anyone who confesses and forsakes them shall receive mercy (Proverbs 28:13). Hence, the moment you confess and forsake your sins the blood of Jesus Christ comes to cleanse and make you whole. This is one thing that the blood of Jesus Christ does.

Sometime ago a young Christian lady came to me for counselling. She had fallen into the sin of immorality. She felt so bad that she was contemplating suicide. After a lengthy time of discussion and

sharing the Scriptures, I succeeded in pointing her to
the blood of Jesus that can cleanse from all sins. She
believed and we prayed together. Immediately her
countenance changed. She became radiant again. The
joy of the Lord was restored to her and she left with a
determination to glorify Jesus all the days of her life.

There is cleansing in the blood of Jesus. If you
have never taken advantage of this blood before, it is
still flowing. By faith you can be cleansed from all
your sins and be holy in God's sight.

4

Power in the Blood

There is mighty power in the blood of Jesus. The power in this precious blood prevails against all satanic and demonic powers and gives victory to every true believer. This is something we must know.

We are involved in spiritual warfare on a daily basis. This is not a battle against flesh and blood, but against malevolent spirits and strong demonic agents. The Bible says:

> For we wrestle not against flesh and blood, but against principalities, against powers, against the rulers of the darkness of this world, against spiri tual wickedness in high places.

Ephesians 6:12

These are the spirits responsible for every evil thing that happens in the world today. They are the enemies of God, enemies of the gospel, enemies of Christians and all righteousness. To be ignorant of their operations and devices is to become their victim. But, thank God, we are not ignorant of the devices of the devil.

While it is true that we are involved daily in spiritual conflicts, God has given us weapons of victory by which we are to overcome the powers of darkness.

> For the weapons of our warfare are not carnal, but

*mighty through God to the pulling down of strong
holds.*

II Corinthians 10:4

The blood of Jesus Christ is one of the mighty
weapons by which we overcome our adversaries.

Power to Protect

The blood of Jesus has power to protect us from all
evil and all attacks of the devil. When you are under
the blood of Jesus Christ the devil cannot do you any
harm. The Bible says:

*He that dwelleth in the secret place of the most High
Shall abide under the shadow of the Almighty.*

Psalm 91:1

Dwelling under the blood of Jesus Christ is dwelling
in the secret place of the Most High.

I often see a small sticker on the doorstep of
Christian homes around Nigeria. It reads: 'This house
is covered by the Blood of Jesus.' This is one way of
acknowledging the protective power of the blood of
Jesus from all evil, and it works. We are to turn our
faith into a confession and use it to whip the devil.
We are to write the Word of God and put it on our
doorposts (Deuteronomy 6:6–9). It is by the word of
our testimony and by the blood of the Lamb that we
overcome the evil one.

When the people of Israel were to be led out of
Egypt by Moses, God showed them in a picture the
power of the blood of Jesus to protect them from
every evil. This was called the Passover. The Lord
was to pass through all Egypt in judgment. There
would be a plague in every home. Every first-born

was to be killed. The Lord then gave the people of Israel a token, a sign of the blood of the Lamb. Each family was to take a lamb, kill and eat it. They were to use the blood to mark the side posts and lintels of their houses. Everywhere the blood was, there was total safety and complete protection. But where there was no blood there was destruction.

> *For I will pass through the land of Egypt this night, and will smite all the firstborn in the land of Egypt, both man and beast; and against all the gods of Egypt I will execute judgment: I am the LORD. And the blood shall be to you for a token upon the houses where ye are: and when I see the blood, I will pass over you, and the plague shall not be upon you to destroy you, when I smite the land of Egypt.*
>
> Exodus 12:12–13

The plague passed through Egypt. There was destruction everywhere except where the blood was. But where the blood was, there was perfect protection.

The blood was actually pointing to the blood of Jesus Christ, the Lamb of God, who shed His blood for us. When we are under the blood, we are safe.

To dwell under the blood of Jesus is to be in the secret place of the Most High. There is sure protection in the blood of Jesus. You can boldly claim and declare your protection from plagues, diseases, accidents, demonic attacks, robberies and violence through the blood of Jesus. And wherever the devil is trying to attack you or your family, boldly plead the blood of Jesus and you will be completely protected. The Bible makes it clear that it is by the blood of the Lamb and the word of our testimony that we overcome the evil one.

One of my brothers experienced this. He lived at Ilorin, in a compound of four flats. One night the Lord woke his wife to pray and plead the blood of Jesus upon their home by faith. My brother was too tired to pray but his wife prayed for a little over an hour before going back to bed. Shortly afterwards, a gang invaded their compound and robbed the other three flats, but theirs was never touched. You may want to explain it away as mere coincidence. Not so. I believe an angel of the Lord took position and shielded their home from the robbers' attack because they trusted in the precious blood of Jesus. Because they were covered by the blood of Jesus, they dwelt in safety. I shall speak about the protective power of the blood in a later chapter.

Victory Now

God has ordained victory for us over the assaults of the enemy. Every believer in Christ is supposed to be 'more than a conqueror'. You are never to be afraid of Satan, or witches or wizards or any of the powers of darkness. You are more than a match for the devil and his hosts because Jesus Christ now lives in you by the Holy Spirit! The Bible says:

> *Ye are of God, little children, and have overcome them: because greater is he that is in you, than he that is in the world.*

> I John 4:4

You should know this as a child of God and be very bold in your victory.

'But,' you say, 'why all these attacks of the devil if I am more than a conqueror?' Satan is in the world to accuse, attack, hinder and do all he can against you, but God has given you a singular weapon of victory: the blood of Jesus Christ.

You do not have to fold your arms and watch the devil attack you with sickness, diseases, lacks, fears, unclean thoughts and the like. Use the blood of Jesus against him. The blood of Jesus will always break the hold of Satan and loose the blessings of God. The blood of Jesus Christ is irresistible to the enemy. The Bible says:

> And they overcame him by the blood of the Lamb, and by the word of their testimony; and they loved not their lives unto the death.

> Revelation 12:11

Note that the scripture says *'they overcame . . .'*

We are **not** to accept defeat and then 'resign ourselves to fate'. We are **not** to accept all that comes as 'the will of God'.

You can boldly claim and declare your protection from plagues, diseases, accidents, demonic attacks, robberies and violence through the blood of Jesus.

Anything that is contrary to the Scriptures; contrary to God's promise of abundant life and health; anything that comes from the devil, must be strongly resisted with the blood of Jesus. Remember, the kingdom of heaven now suffers violence and the violent one takes it by force. If we resist the devil, the Bible says, *'he will flee'* from us (James 4:7). One way we can effectively put him to flight is by the blood of Jesus.

There was a young believer in Ibadan who by faith

in the Word of God changed his situation academically, socially and financially. I met him in 1977. He had failed the School Certificate examinations woefully before becoming a believer. On getting saved, having been taught that if any man is in Christ he is a new creature, he decided to re-sit his exams. His parents urged him not to. 'When you were in school and had all the teachers you failed,' they said. 'Now that you are out of school do you think you will succeed as an external candidate?' 'I believe God. I am now a new creation,' he replied. He re-sat the examination and passed his eight papers in one go. He applied for the Advanced Level papers and passed three. With that he went to the University of Lagos to read Law. Today, he has a flourishing law chamber in Lagos. This is a case of the stone which the builders rejected becoming the main conerstone. The Word of God will change your entire being and you will be what God wants you to be.

Russia Experience

In 1994, our ministry called a Pastor/Leaders conference in Russia. We had close to two thousand people participating over five days. What a glorious time we had in the presence of the Lord. But the first night of the meeting was a disaster. I was preaching and the heaven was oppressive like brass. We could sense a strong demonic influence over the meeting; so that night I stayed up to pray and resist the prince of darkness in that area with the blood. Early the following morning, the whole ministry team spent one solid hour in warfare intercession, and there was a breakthrough. You only need to see how the meeting went that day. Our family friends, Pastor Tony and

Margaret Cornell from Ely in England ministered. There was such a release of grace upon the meeting. The Holy Spirit moved powerfully and it was like that all through the conference. How did the victory come? By the blood of the Lamb. Glory to His holy name.

Anything that is contrary to the Scriptures; contrary to God's promise of abundant life and health; anything that comes from the devil, must be strongly resisted with the blood of Jesus.

Whenever I am dealing with a tough demonic case or having a confrontation with the powers of darkness, I plead the blood of Jesus.

There have been instances when I have perceived demonic forces against our meetings hindering the flow of the anointing and blessings of God. At such times I plead the blood of Jesus and command the demons to depart. And they have obeyed. These are just some practical examples.

The blood of Jesus is powerful. We are to plead it against the devil whenever he brings an attack against us. In any aspect of our lives, victory is certain by the blood of Jesus.

Prevailing Prayer

One practical area where the blood of Jesus gives total victory is in prayer. The hour of prayer is the hour of power. The devil knows this and often tries to disturb our prayers and fellowship with God.

Here you are, wanting to really pray, but heaven is like brass. Everything is dry; there is no breakthrough at all. Know that the enemy is at work. Plead the blood of Jesus against all demons that are trying to hinder your prayer. As you boldly plead the blood, there will be a release of divine grace and power and you will have your breakthrough in prayer.

Very few Christians realize that the hour of prayer is the hour of conflict. It is the time we engage the hosts of hell in a duel. We have heard so much about the possibilities of prayer. We have read so much about great exploits we can do by prayer.

Each time we read the account of our Lord's life in the Gospels we yearn to pray as He did. But why are we so disinclined to prayer? Why do we feel weak, dizzy, sleepy and weary with all sorts of wandering thoughts floating in our minds when we come to prayer? Why are there so many demonically organized natural interruptions at the time we really want to pray? It is the time the telephone chooses to ring again and again. It is the time important but unscheduled visitors decide to call. It is the time some members of the family need our attention urgently. Why then?

We must know that there are demonic forces set against us to stop us from praying or to hinder the answers. In the face of these, are we to accept defeat? Never. We have the blood of Jesus. At those times when you perceive that the enemy is trying to hinder your prayer in any form, plead the blood of Jesus.

Personally, my prayer times that started dull, dry and uninteresting have become very warm, powerful and inspiring, because I took advantage of the blood of Jesus to overcome all demonic hosts.

In 1992, we were in the city of Makurdi for a crusade. It was to last five days. We had prayed with

fasting and our team had worked tirelessly to mobi-
lize the entire city. The first day, I was in the presence
of the Lord getting ready for the meeting that night. I
felt so empty, so light, I just could not pray. While I
was still struggling, my ministerial assistant came in
to inform me that a bishop in the city was dying of
cancer and he had sent some of his pastors to ask me
to pray that he might be healed. The message put
such a heavy burden on my heart. I began to pray and
weep, pleading the blood of Jesus very fervently. I
prayed with the spirit and also with understanding. I
was in that state for three full hours. And the Lord
gave me a clear breakthrough, not just about the bishop but about the meeting that evening – which will
not be forgotten in a hurry. The word came so powerfully. People got soundly born again. There were so
many testimonies of healings and miracles. The
breakthrough came by the blood of the Lamb.

The tremendous power in the blood of Jesus is
available to you today. It has power to save, heal,
deliver and set free completely. Through the blood of
Jesus your victory is as sure as the throne of God.

Enjoying the Full Benefit of Our Redemption

The redemption Jesus brought for us by His blood is
full and complete. He has come to redeem us from all
sins so that we can be 'peculiar' people, set aside for
Him, holy unto God. The Bible talks of Jesus Christ;

> Who gave himself for us [or shed his blood for us],
> that he might redeem us from all iniquity, and
> purify unto himself a peculiar people, zealous of
> good works.

>   Titus 2:14

He also came to redeem us from all the powers of darkness. This simply means He has set us free from Satan and all forms of demonic oppression by His blood. God our Father is spoken of as having *'delivered us from the power of darkness, and hath translated us into the kingdom of his dear Son: in whom we have redemption through his blood, even the forgiveness of sins'* (Colossians 1:13–14). Hence our redemption includes total liberty from all demonic torments whether mental or physical, emotional or any other.

Note this also: Jesus Christ has redeemed us from sicknesses and diseases by His blood that He shed. The Bible is very clear on this, that our physical healing is contained in the atonement. Sickness is part of the effect of sin on the human race. The atonement that dealt with the cause definitely takes care of the effect.

> *Surely he hath borne our griefs, and carried our sorrows; yet we did esteem him stricken: smitten of God, and afflicted. But he was wounded for our transgressions, he was bruised for our iniquities: the chastisement of our peace was upon him; and with his stripes we are healed.*
>
> Isaiah 53:4,5

We are also redeemed from poverty. One of the rods of destruction in the hands of the devil is poverty. God did not make us poor and He never intended for us to be poor at any time. He made us in His image, put us in His garden of abundance and put the whole world and its resources at our

Through the blood of Jesus your victory is as sure as the throne of God.

disposal. But with the fall came poverty and the
human race has been struggling with it ever since.

Jesus Christ came, identified with our poverty and
lifted us out of it. The Bible says:

*For ye know the grace of our Lord Jesus Christ, that,
though he was rich, yet for your sakes he became
poor, that ye through his poverty might be rich.*

II Corinthians 8:9

One of the effects of the gospel of Jesus is that it
delivers people from poverty and brings them into
abundance. He Himself said *'I am come that they might
have life, and that they might have it more abundantly'*
(John 10:10).

Now you can enjoy the full benefits of our
redemption in Christ.

The devil, certainly, will want to keep you away
from these blessings for as long as he can, but you do
not need to allow him to a single day longer. Resist
him by the blood of Jesus, claim your victory and
start to enjoy your full redemption. The salvation of
God is so full and free. You have been redeemed from
sin, Satan, sickness, poverty and all the curses of the
law through the precious blood of Jesus.

When Jesus Christ was brought before Pontius
Pilate, Pilate ordered that the Lord should be beaten.
He was so thoroughly beaten that His body was
badly bruised. Then the soldiers that beat him put a
crown of thorns on his head. In the process of all this
His blood flowed.

*Then Pilate therefore took Jesus, and scourged him.
And the soldiers platted a crown of thorns, and put
it on his head, and they put on him a purple robe.*

John 19:1–2

*Just as there were many who were appalled at him –
his appearance was so disfigured beyond that of
    any man
and his form marred beyond human likeness . . .*
                                    Isaiah 52:14 (NIV)

Also when the Roman soldiers went to find out
whether the people on the cross had died (that is, our
Lord Jesus and the two thieves crucified along with
Him), they saw that Jesus had, but to be doubly sure,
one of them plunged a spear into our Lord's side.
From that side, blood and water gushed out. *'But one
of the soldiers with a spear pierced his side, and forthwith
came there out blood and water'* (John 19:34).

Why all this? The Lord was fulfilling prophecies.
By shedding His blood, and suffering such agonies,
He bore our sicknesses and diseases on His own
body, *'that it might be fulfilled which was spoken by
Esaias the prophet, saying, Himself took our infirmities,
and bare our sicknesses'* (Matthew 8:17).

By putting your faith in Him, and in His name
boldly claiming your healing by faith, His blood can
set you free at once from any sickness, no matter how
chronic or terrible.

Our complete redemption is more fully explored
later in this book. But for now know it within your
heart that there is power in the blood of Jesus:

- to release you from every stronghold of the devil.
- to protect you from all the onslaught of Satan.
- to give you absolute victory in the midst of every
  storm.
- to give you complete breakthrough in prayer.
- to release for your enjoyment all the benefits of
  our complete redemption in Christ Jesus.
- to make you a winner on the face of the earth.

5

The Blood of Life

Blood is sacred . . . it flows from God. No man can manufacture blood. It is of God.

Blood is life. The life of every animal is in the blood.

God says, 'The life of the flesh is in the blood' (Leviticus 17:11).

If you want to kill a man, drain his blood. As soon as it is drained the man is gone. When people are critically ill or have lost a lot of blood, a blood transfusion is carried out. The man is transfused with another man's blood and he lives again.

But there is something peculiar about the blood of Jesus. It contains not just animal life but the very life of God, eternal life. When we are 'transfused' with the blood of Jesus Christ through faith we receive the very life of God and live like God intended us to. Alleluia!

You may be in a critical spiritual condition right now. Perhaps you are cast down and the adversary thinks you are finished. Men seeing your situation may also rule out the possibility of your survival. Look to the Lamb of God. Just a dose of the precious blood of Jesus Christ through faith and your situation is completely turned around.

Now listen, beloved. Through the precious blood of Jesus you are a champion for God. Like Edwin

Louis Cole once said, champions are not those who never fail, they are those who never quit. In case the enemy has ruled out the possibility of your survival and has laughed at you with scorn, through the blood of Jesus this is your song of faith:

> *Therefore I will look unto the LORD; I will wait for the God of my salvation: my God will hear me. Rejoice not against me, O mine enemy: when I fall, I shall arise; when I sit in darkness, the LORD shall be a light unto me . . . Then she that is mine enemy shall see it, and shame shall cover her which said unto me, Where is the LORD thy God? mine eyes shall behold her: now shall she be trodden down as the mire of the streets.*

Micah 7:7, 8, 10

Absolutely Perfect

There are four main blood groups people have: A, AB, B, or O. They must be transfused only with their own blood group, otherwise they die. The blood group O, however, can be used for anyone, regardless of his or her blood group. It is the universal donor. People with that particular blood group are always sought after to donate blood for use in case of an emergency. However, this is not medically ideal, because it is not free of complications – the ideal is to transfuse with the exactly compatible blood group.

Thanks be to God, for the blood of Jesus Christ matches all human blood groups. By receiving the redemption that is in that blood you are delivered from sin and shame, you are delivered from death and destruction, and you receive the abundant life that Jesus has brought for us. And there are no complications of any kind! The blood of Jesus Christ is the perfect solution to all human and spiritual malaise. By it we receive life, even abundant life.

Thanks be to God, for the blood of Jesus Christ matches all human blood groups. By receiving the redemption that is in that blood you are delivered from sin and shame . . . from death and destruction, and you receive the abundant life that Jesus has brought for us.

The thief cometh not, but for to steal, and to kill, and to destroy: I am come that they might have life, and that they might have it more abundantly.

John 10:10

There was a case sometime ago of a young lady from a Muslim family who was critically ill at the University College Hospital in Ibadan. She was bleeding so badly the doctors were afraid she might die. They decided to give her a transfusion but it only increased the rate of her blood loss. We got to hear about her and I sent one of our pastors to go and minister to her. He said the Holy Spirit led him to lay hands on her and plead the blood of Jesus. Within five minutes the blood flow stopped completely. The lady was healed and she received Jesus as her Saviour and Lord. In spite of all the persecution that broke out against her, she is still serving the Lord Jesus steadfastly today. There is power in the blood of Jesus.

What Jesus Said

Jesus Christ said some things about His blood which

are very important for us to know, understand and appropriate by faith.

> *Then Jesus said unto them, Verily, verily, I say unto you, Except ye eat the flesh of the Son of man, and drink his blood, ye have no life in you. Whoso eateth my flesh, and drinketh my blood, hath eternal life; and I will raise him up at the last day. For my flesh is meat indeed, and my blood is drink indeed. He that eateth my flesh, and drinketh my blood, dwelleth in me, and I in him. As the living Father hath sent me, and I live by the Father: so he that eateth me, even he shall live by me.*
>
> John 6:53–57

Please note that it is vital to drink the blood of Jesus Christ in order to have life. Nobody really has eternal life unless he has partaken of that blood. Also, when you drink of the blood of Jesus there is the quickening of all your faculties. You receive God's vibrant life into your being.

I remember an experience I had sometime in 1985. I had just concluded a ten-day crusade at Oyo, in Nigeria. (Those were days of marathon crusades. Sometimes we went on for weeks in a single city until the entire city was stirred for Jesus.) I then went straight on to Lagos to speak at a convention running another week. It was a time of intense ministrations and at the end of it I was physically quite exhausted. In my spirit I was strong but in my body I was tired and weary.

I then travelled to Ibadan to attend a wedding that I had promised to go to. The celebration of the Lord's Supper was part of the wedding. I was really glad. All my being was crying out for the body of the Lord and His blood, symbolized by the bread and wine. There was a witness inside me that by partaking of the Lord's Table, I would be revived and strengthened. I prepared my heart and went forward. I was so quickened both physically and spiritually that I was able to go through another week of vigorous ministry. This experience made such an impact on me that I came to realize again that indeed divine life flows in the blood of Jesus. When you approach the Lord's Table, make sure you go in faith to receive divine life for your entire being – spirit, soul and body.

Physical healing and deliverance flows too, as we partake of the blood of Jesus.

Remember that His blood was shed to redeem us from the curses of the law. As we partake of the blood, sickness and diseases, which are major parts of the curse, leave as we appropriate His blessings by faith.

It has happened in our ministry that several times while ministering the Lord's Supper to God's people, many have confessed that they received their bodily healing too.

In the scriptures quoted above Jesus mentioned some very crucial blessings that are yours because you partake of His body and blood:

- You live in Him and He lives in you.
- You have His life in you . . . eternal life.
- You shall be raised on the resurrection morning.
- You shall live by Him.

These are crucial.

Except Christ is in you and you are in Christ you have no hope at all.

Which is Christ in you, the hope of glory.

Colossians 1:27

Through the blood of Jesus you have the life of God embedded in you.

No man has life by himself. We all live by God. Every Christian has the seed of God in him, the life of God which is incorruptible. Your body may be wearing out, but the life of God in you is unaffected. When you die, your body may be buried and eaten up by worms but God's life in you remains intact; eternal in the presence of God.

For example, a grain of corn that is vibrant has inside it the embryo as well as the endosperm. The endosperm may be eaten by worms, but so long as the embryo is untouched the seed will still germinate.

For those who have received life by the blood of Jesus the resurrection morning will soon dawn. Our mortal body shall be changed into the exact image of Jesus Christ, we shall be raised incorruptible and we shall live and reign forever with Jesus Christ. This is our hope, by the blood of Jesus.

'Whoso eateth my flesh, and drinketh my blood, hath eternal life; and I will raise him up at the last day.'

John 6:54

How Do You Drink the Blood?

When you receive Jesus Christ by faith as your Saviour and Lord and appropriate the blessings in His blood, you are drinking of this blood of life. If you have not done that, do it right now.

Secondly, you take the blood of Jesus Christ when you partake of the Lord's Supper. This is a sacred ordinance instituted by Jesus Christ Himself to be partaken by every believer from time to time.

Lastly, as you feed on the Word of God, you are drinking of the blood of Jesus Christ and eating His flesh by faith. He is the Living Word of God. Let us continue to feed on the bread of life and drink of the blood of life until we see Jesus our Lord face to face.

This is why it is important for every Christian to nourish himself or herself daily in the Word of God. As you study and meditate on it God speaks to you. Your inner man is strengthened and built up. You become strong spiritually, able to do exploits and reflect the glory of God. Every believer who has taken time to meditate in the Scriptures can testify to the refreshing power of the Word of God.

> *It is important for every Christian to nourish himself or herself daily in the Word of God. As you study and meditate on it God speaks to you. Your inner man is strengthened and built up.*

As a matter of fact one of the means Jesus has ordained by which to continuously cleanse and renew His Church is the Word of God. Therefore, as a believer, each time you dwell in His Word, it answers to the blood and you grow into the likeness of Christ.

You are transformed into His likeness from glory to glory:

> *But we all, with open face beholding as in a glass the glory of the Lord, are changed into the same image from glory to glory, even as by the Spirit of the Lord.*
> II Corinthians 3:18

You are purged and cleansed of all filth and sin:

> *'Sanctify them through thy truth: thy word is truth.'*
>
> John 17:17

You are sanctified and preserved. Every spot and wrinkle in your life is effectively taken care of.

> *Husbands, love your wives, even as Christ also loved the church, and gave himself for it; that he might sanctify and cleanse it with the washing of water by the word, that he might present it to himself a glorious church, not having spot, or wrinkle, or any such thing; but that it should be holy and without blemish.*
>
> Ephesians 5:25–27

You are strengthened greatly in the inner man by His Spirit:

> *That Christ may dwell in your hearts by faith; that ye, being rooted and grounded in love, may be able to comprehend with all saints what is the breadth, and length, and depth, and height; and to know the love of Christ, which passeth knowledge, that ye might be filled with all the fulness of God.*
>
> Ephesians 3:17–19

You receive His wisdom, you partake of His understanding and His insight:

> *I have more understanding than all my teachers: for thy testimonies are my meditation.*
> *I understand more than the ancients, because I keep thy precepts.*
>
> Psalm 119:99–100

You are given direct divine instructions as to the what, the how, the where, the when and the who of the plan of God for your life:

Thy word is a lamp unto my feet, and a light unto my path.

Psalm 119:105

You are warned of impending danger and led by the Holy Spirit to avoid them:

Moreover by them is thy servant warned: and in keeping of them there is great reward.

Psalm 19:11

You receive divine ability to act wisely and to succeed in everything you lay your hands on:

But his delight is in the law of the LORD; and in his law doth he meditate day and night. And he shall be like a tree planted by the rivers of water, that bringeth forth his fruit in his season; his leaf also shall not wither; and whatsoever he doeth shall prosper.

Psalm 1:2–3

You are loaded with all the goodness of God so that you may be a blessing to others:

This book of the law shall not depart out of thy mouth; but thou shalt meditate therein day and night, that thou mayest observe to do according to all that is written therein: for then thou shalt make thy way prosperous, and then thou shalt have good success.

Joshua 1:8

You are built up greatly and abundantly edified. You are given your own portion of the inheritance of the saints in light.

> *And now, brethren, I commend you to God, and to the word of his grace, which is able to build you up, and to give you an inheritance among all them which are sanctified.*
>
> Acts 20:32

Let us daily feed on this living bread. It will make the difference between success and failure, between wisdom and folly, between health and sickness, between life and death.

6

The Blood – Our Stronghold

When we talk about spiritual strongholds, many believers immediately think of the negative; and the verses of Scripture that readily come to mind are in second Corinthians, chapter 10.

> *For though we walk in the flesh, we do not war after the flesh: (for the weapons of our warfare are not carnal, but mighty through God to the pulling down of strong holds;) casting down imaginations, and every high thing that exalteth itself against the knowledge of God, and bringing into captivity every thought to the obedience of Christ.*
>
> II Corinthians 10:3–5

Because the Bible says we should pull down strongholds by using our weapons of spiritual warfare, we assume every stronghold must be satanic, and must be pulled down. The same thing goes with the subject of principalities and powers based on our understanding of Ephesians 6:10–18. Remember, Satan is an arch-counterfeiter! He only tries to imitate what God does. If there are satanic strongholds to pull down, then there must be divine strongholds where there is the power to pull down all the satanic strongholds, just as there are angelic principalities and powers who aid us in defeating demonic principalities and powers.

What is a stronghold? A stronghold is a place of fortified defence, impenetrable to the adversary. When battles get tough people run into their stronghold. If you can get hold of them before they enter into the stronghold, fine. If not, the moment they enter in, you can no longer get them. They become invincible. And from that place of their strength, they wreak havoc and devastate their adversaries.

God has established the blood of Jesus Christ as our stronghold. It is both a place of strong defence and a powerful, irresistible weapon of spiritual warfare. That is why God urges us to turn to our stronghold and from there devour and destroy the adversary:

> *As for thee also, by the blood of thy covenant I have sent forth thy prisoners out of the pit wherein is no water. Turn you to the strong hold, ye prisoners of hope: even to day do I declare that I will render double unto thee.*
>
> Zechariah 9:11–12

When a believer stays under the cover of the blood of Jesus Christ by faith, he is completely covered, safe from all harm for time and eternity. The most secure place of refuge God has provided for us is under the blood of Jesus Christ the Lamb of God. Whatever weapon of attack the enemy directs at you is frustrated when you stay under the cover of the blood. It is the secret place of the Most High, under the shadow of the Almighty.

> *He that dwelleth in the secret place of the most High*
> *Shall abide under the shadow of the Almighty.*
> *I will say of the LORD, He is my refuge and*
> *my fortress:*

My God; in him will I trust.
                                    Psalm 91:1–2

Most Bible scholars believe that Moses wrote that
psalm during the time of the Passover in Egypt,
which I talked about earlier in
this book, when God was visiting Egypt with judgment and
there was death in every house
except the houses of the people
of Israel who put the blood of a
lamb on their doorpost. Their
houses were not to be visited by
the angel of destruction because
through the blood of the lamb
they had become the secret
places of the Most High.
Anyone who stayed under the
blood was safe. It was a picture
of the blood of Jesus, the perfect
Lamb of God. The blood of Jesus marks out the real
secret place of the Most High.

*If there are satanic
strongholds to pull
down, then there
must be divine
strongholds where
there is the power
to pull down
all satanic
strongholds.*

Remember, the life of the flesh is in the blood.
When you are covered by the blood of Jesus you are
covered by His very life. Then is your life *'hid with
Christ in God'* (Colossians 3:3). Then you are not living
your own life anymore; you live by the faith of the
Son of God who loves you and gave Himself for you.

*For ye are dead, and your life is hid with Christ in
God.*

                                    Colossians 3:3

The blood of Jesus is the place of defence God has
established for us so that we can be far from terror
and oppression. Not only does the blood cleanse us

from sin continually as we abide under it, it keeps us safe from all potential dangers and threats of the enemy.

> *But if we walk in the light, as he is in the light, we have fellowship one with another, and the blood of Jesus Christ his Son cleanseth us from all sin.*
>
> I John 1:7

The blood of Jesus . . . that is the place of your defence! That is the place of your stronghold!

> *He shall dwell on high: his place of defence shall be the munitions of rocks: bread shall be given him; his waters shall be sure.*
> *Thine eyes shall see the king in his beauty: they shall behold the land that is very far off.*
>
> Isaiah 33:16–17

When God was visiting Egypt with judgment, He asked His people to remain under the blood of the lamb that had become their stronghold. Wherever the blood was, the angel of destruction could not enter; the blood kept him off. Everywhere the blood was not found there was destruction, death, wailing and gnashing of teeth. But the Israelites found their stronghold under the blood and they were safe and secure from all harm.

The blood still works in exactly the same way today. There is so much evil in our world: crimes, violence, abuse, destruction. The Bible speaks of '*the terror by night . . . the arrow that flieth by day . . . the pestilence that walketh in darkness . . . the destruction that wasteth at noonday*' (Psalm 91:5–6). These are agents of the devil, sent forth to steal, to kill and to destroy.

But for those who are under the cover of the blood

of Jesus by faith, God's word of promise rings with
certain assurance:

> *The blood of Jesus
> is the place of
> defence God has
> established for
> us so that we
> can be far from
> terror and
> oppression. Not
> only does the
> blood cleanse
> us from sin
> continually as
> we abide under
> it, it keeps us safe
> from all potential
> dangers and
> threats of the
> enemy.*

*He shall cover thee with his
feathers,
And under his wings shalt thou
trust:
His truth shall be thy shield and
buckler . . .
A thousand shall fall at thy side,
And ten thousand at thy right
hand;
But it shall not come nigh thee.
Only with thine eyes shalt thou
behold
And see the reward of the
wicked.
Because thou hast made the
LORD, which is my refuge,
Even the most High, thy
habitation;
There shall no evil befall thee,
Neither shall any plague come
nigh thy dwelling.*

Psalm 91:4, 7–10

How does a man make the Lord his refuge and his
habitation? By staying by faith under the cover of the
blood of Jesus Christ the Lamb of God.

May I sound this warning? There is nothing for
you to trust as a defence that is as reliable, as the
blood of Jesus. Every arm of flesh will fail. No charm,
juju, occult power, talisman or any human defence
will work. Human connection is feeble. There are

days that even strong relationships do not work. If you do not put your trust in the blood of the Lamb and in the name of the Lord, sooner or later something will break down and your defence will fail you.

Some trust in chariots, and some in horses:
But we will remember the name of the LORD our
  God.
They are brought down and fallen:
But we are risen, and stand upright.
                                   Psalm 20:7–8

I have spoken of our stronghold as a place of defence, and it certainly is. The blood of Jesus is a place of stronghold from where we pull down other strongholds – those of the devil. You become extremely effective in spiritual warfare when you abide under the cover of the blood of Jesus Christ. You become a sharpshooter for God. You are able to deal effectively with the powers of darkness and vanquish them, setting men and women free from the strongholds of the enemy.

Let me share an example with you. There was a time when the Philistines effectively blocked David from reaching the place of his heart's desire. He wanted water so badly. It was available in abundance at the well of Bethlehem. But that was where the enemy had established their garrison, their stronghold.

David knew he could not deal with the enemy's stronghold unless he himself got into his own stronghold. So he moved into his stronghold and from there launched an offensive against the adversary. He routed the enemies and got a breakthrough into his heart's desire. Read the story:

And David was then in an hold, and the garrison of

*the Philistines was then in Beth-lehem. And David
longed, and said, Oh that one would give me drink
of the water of the well of Beth-lehem, which is by
the gate! And the three mighty men brake through
the host of the Philistines, and drew water out of the
well of Beth-lehem, that was by the gate, and took it,
and brought it to David: nevertheless he would not
drink thereof, but poured it out unto the* LORD. *And
he said, Be it far from me, O* LORD, *that I should do
this: is not this the blood of the men that went in
jeopardy of their lives? therefore he would not drink
it. These things did these three mighty men.*

II Samuel 23:14–17

David had a mighty victory over the stronghold of
the enemy because he moved into his own stronghold. It was a battle of gods. Stronghold against
stronghold. Rock against rock. But our Rock is higher
than their rock, our stronghold is stronger than their
stronghold. Our God is the ruler of the whole universe, the Governor among the nations. Our God
reigns. Alleluia!

You will get into certain situations in life that if
God does not take over you are finished. But if Jesus
is truly your Lord, and God Almighty is truly your
Father, then you have no problem. Just trust Him and
turn the battle over to Him. He will deal with the
adversaries and you will be sorry for them.

You may often have to retreat into your stronghold
like David did. It is foolishness to continue to fight
when you know that tactical withdrawal is what will
give you the victory. Many times our Lord Jesus with-
drew from the crowd and went into a place of prayer
retreat. David Yonggi Cho has a special place he
always withdraws into to pray, to seek God's face in

order to pull down the stronghold of the enemy. Are you getting weary in the battle already? Withdraw! Get into your stronghold and pray your way into breakthrough, by the blood of the Lamb.

Beloved, get into your stronghold and from there pull down the enemy's strongholds. Let me assure you by the Word of God: they that are for you are more than they that are against you. And greater is He that is in you than he that is in the world. Your stronghold is stronger than their stronghold. Your Rock is higher than their rock. Alleluia. From the place of your stronghold, you are more than a conqueror.

> *Ye are of God, little children, and have overcome them: because greater is he that is in you, than he that is in the world.*
>
> I John 4:4

7

Cleansing the Leper

Leprosy is a terrible, contagious disease. In biblical times there was no known cure. Whenever a man became leprous, he was separated from the rest of the society until the day of his death.

Three Basic Facts about Leprosy

First, leprosy is spiritual. It depicts the ugly and terrible nature of sin and its unalterability by human efforts. According to the revelation of Old Testament Scriptures, *leprosy was a sign of divine disfavour upon a man*.

When Aaron and Miriam spoke against God's servant, Moses, the Lord was displeased and angry. After God had finished speaking with them, Miriam became leprous, white as snow (Numbers 12:10). It was only after God was appeased, as a result of Moses' intercession, that she was cured (Numbers 12:13–15).

Leprosy was a sign of divine judgment. When King Uzziah became strong, his heart became proud and he intruded into the office of the high priest; he went into the temple to burn incense to God. The priests corrected him, but rather than taking the correction he took offence and became angry. God judged him by giving him leprosy from which he never recovered (II Chronicles 26:23).

Leprosy is a picture of the alienation that sin produces between man and God. A leprous man is unclean. A sinful man is unclean before God. Leprosy, therefore, is a perfect picture of sin and its awful defilement.

He is a leprous man, he is unclean: the priest shall pronounce him utterly unclean; his plague is in his head. And the leper in whom the plague is, his clothes shall be rent, and his head bare, and he shall put a covering upon his upper lip, and shall cry, Unclean, unclean. All the days wherein the plague shall be in him he shall be defiled; he is unclean: he shall dwell alone; without the camp shall his habitation be.

Leviticus 13:44–46

Secondly, leprosy is social in nature. It puts a social stigma upon whoever it affects. As soon as a man becomes leprous he is separated from the rest of the people. He is considered unclean and dangerous because of this contagious disease. In Israel, the leper had to go outside the camp and not mix with the rest of the people throughout Israel's journey through the wilderness.

When Israel settled in the land God gave them, the law still prevailed. The leper was to be camped outside the city. By law, he was required to tie little bells around the hem of his clothes which would jingle as he walked along the road. As the bells rang, the leper would shout, 'Unclean! Unclean!' to alert people coming along so they could steer clear of him. To be leprous was a terrible shame and humiliation. It meant being stigmatized and isolated, taunted and unwelcome. A leper suffered terrible rejection.

Thirdly, leprosy is a terrible physical disease.

The flesh rots and degenerates. The skin becomes whitish. Fingers and limbs wear away until they become mere stumps. Terrible physical deformities and disabilities are the end-products of leprosy.

Therefore, when a man becomes leprous, he suffers spiritually, socially and physically.

Obedience Produced Healing

In those days when there was no known cure for leprosy, God provided means whereby His covenant people might be healed and cleansed from this plague. The leper only needed to be obedient to the priests and the instructions they gave him from God's word. Obedience was what was needed. The instructions given might appear senseless and without meaning; the details might beat any logical explanation; yet that was what God prescribed for complete healing and cleansing. Any leper that obeyed was healed and cleansed. Anyone who refused to obey died leprous.

Throughout the Scriptures, we see God giving people instructions that appear neither sensible nor logical. Imagine God telling an Israelite bitten by a serpent in the wilderness to look at the brazen serpent upon the pole in order to be healed! Imagine the consternation of Naaman when God's prophet told him to go and dip himself in the River Jordan seven times to be cleansed of his leprosy! Imagine the confusion of Mary when the angel told her she was going to conceive and have a son when she was still a virgin!

What God requires of His people in order to be healed and blessed is faith and obedience. As the old song says, 'Trust and obey', that is all you have to do to be happy in Jesus.

Let us now look at the book of Leviticus chapter 14 to find God's instruction for the cleansing of the leper. The first seven verses, interestingly, are one long single sentence, showing that even though several items are mentioned in the verses, there is only one message.

And the LORD spake unto Moses, saying, This shall be the law of the leper in the day of his cleansing: He shall be brought unto the priest: and the priest shall go forth out of the camp; and the priest shall look, and, behold, if the plague of leprosy be healed in the leper; then shall the priest command to take for him that is to be cleansed two birds alive and clean, and cedar wood, and scarlet, and hyssop: and the priest shall command that one of the birds be killed in an earthen vessel over running water: as for the living bird, he shall take it, and the cedar wood, and the scarlet, and the hyssop, and shall dip them and the living bird in the blood of the bird that was killed over the running water: and he shall sprinkle upon him that is to be cleansed from the leprosy seven times, and shall pronounce him clean, and shall let the living bird loose into the open field.

Leviticus 14:1–7

These are physical things that God was using to illustrate the spiritual. The Bible says '. . . *the law having a shadow of good things to come* . . .' (Hebrews 10:1).

Which are a shadow of things to come; but the body is of Christ.

Colossians 2:17

We can understand here that the law of the Old

84 THE PRECIOUS BLOOD OF JESUS

Testament is a shadow of what was to come; Jesus Christ is the substance that was represented by the shadow. He is the fulfilment of the law and the prophets.

Notice that it took one day for the leper to be cleansed. This passage speaks of *'in the day of his cleansing'* (v 1). Unlike man-made religions which teach that it takes long years of good works to achieve harmony with God, the gospel teaches that it takes only one day to be cleansed from our sin by the blood of Jesus Christ. The consequences of a sin may linger, the scar may abide for the rest of the sinner's life, the punishment may be prolonged, but God forgives and cleanses the very moment repentance is thorough and genuine

What God requires of His people in order to be healed and blessed is faith and obedience. As the old song says, 'Trust and obey', that is all you have to do to be happy in Jesus.

Notice the two attributes of the birds to be used in the cleansing: **alive** and **clean.**

These two birds depict Christ. One would be killed and the blood shed to symbolize the crucifixion of Christ. The other was left alive to symbolize His resurrection. Just as Jesus Christ is alive and blameless, the birds were to be alive and clean.

The cedar wood symbolizes the cross upon which Jesus was crucified and the scarlet material symbolizes atonement by the blood of Jesus Christ.

The hyssop that was used to transfer the blood represents faith. It is by faith the blood is obtained and applied.

The earthen vessel represents the body of our Lord Jesus that was bruised before the blood could be shed.

The running water is a shadow of 'the eternal Spirit' through whom Jesus offered His precious blood.

> *How much more shall the blood of Christ, who through the eternal Spirit offered himself without spot to God, purge your conscience from dead works to serve the living God?*
>
> Hebrews 9:14

The leper is to be sprinkled with the blood seven times. Seven in the Bible is the number of perfection or completeness. After the leper is sprinkled seven times, he is pronounced clean. What a day of joy for him! He is clean and whole for ever.

The Blood Applied

This is the application of the word of the Lord. There are two key things that happened to a leper in those days after obeying this divine instruction. He was **healed** and **cleansed**. These two blessings are made available to man through the blood of Jesus Christ our Lord. Let me examine them in reverse.

Cleansing

Sin separates a man from God. Sin defiles and renders a man unclean. *'The wages of sin is death'* (Romans 6:23). If the blood of Jesus is not applied by faith and in complete obedience to the gospel, the soul that sins shall die (Ezekiel 18:4).

But God has caused Jesus Christ to die for our sins; the just for the unjust. He shed His precious blood to make us whole. He offered His blood to God through the eternal Spirit as the remedy for our sins. Anyone who applies that blood by faith shall be cleansed and made whole, as a leper who was healed of the plague of his sin the same day. Just trust and obey and you will be completely all right.

> *Come now, and let us reason together, saith the LORD: though your sins be as scarlet, they shall be as white as snow; though they be red like crimson, they shall be as wool. If ye be willing and obedient, ye shall eat the good of the land..*
>
> Isaiah 1:18–19

Healing

The Bible passage quoted earlier in Leviticus refers to the healing of the leper: *'Behold, if the plague of leprosy be healed in the leper'* (Leviticus 14:3).

God had provided a cure for His people. As they obeyed His Word and His anointed servants in applying the blood, they would experience complete healing.

Even today, there is power in the blood of Jesus to cure every known plague, including those considered medically incurable. Just release your faith in the blood of Jesus and you will be made completely whole. By shedding His precious blood, Jesus paid the price to make you whole, spirit, soul and body.

> *Surely he hath borne our griefs, and carried our sorrows: yet we did esteem him stricken, smitten of God, and afflicted. But he was wounded for our transgressions, he was bruised for our iniquities: the chastisement of our peace was upon him; and with his stripes we are healed.*
>
> Isaiah 53:4–5

Naaman the Leper

This was the experience of Naaman, captain of the Syrian army in those days. He was a leper.

He was told that the God of Israel could make him whole and free him from his leprosy. So he went to the king of Israel, who was totally ignorant of divine healing. The king even thought it was a ploy to start another war. Deliverance is not found in the palace of the king.

When Elisha, God's anointed servant, heard of Naaman's case, he called for him from the palace of the king of Israel, '*Let him come now to me*,' Elisha said, '*. . . and he shall know that there is a prophet in Israel*' (II Kings 5:8). It is the anointing that destroys the yoke. God's authentic prophet will do with ease what kings and rulers cannot do. Not by might nor by power, but by the Spirit of the Lord.

By the inspiration of God, Elisha told Naaman what to do to be whole:

> *. . . Go and wash in Jordan seven times, and thy flesh shall come again to thee, and thou shalt be clean.*

> II Kings 5:10

Even today, there is power in the blood of Jesus to cure every known plague, including those considered medically incurable.

Notice two things Elisha said would happen to Naaman. First, his flesh would come back to him; that is complete healing. Then he was going to be clean.

Dipping in the River Jordan seven times was a picture of the blood of Jesus Christ that cleanses and makes whole.

Of course, the instruction sounded foolish to Naaman. *'Are not Abana and Pharpar, rivers of Damascus, better than all the waters of Israel?'* (II Kings 5:12). Naaman was enraged.

Men always think they have better ideas than God. Good intentions. Self-efforts. Self-righteousness. Fasting. Praying. 'Are these not better than all this "blood" stuff you are telling me?' That is always the reasoning of man. But the foolishness of God is wiser than men, and the weakness of God is stronger than men (I Corinthians 1:25). All that is needed is faith to act on God's Word and the result will be a miracle.

Eventually Naaman was persuaded to obey the words of the prophet. And he got the breakthrough of his life:

> *Then went he down, and dipped himself seven times in Jordan, according to the saying of the man of God: and his flesh came again like unto the flesh of a little child, and he was clean.*

> II Kings 5:14

Notice please, that the two things the prophet of God said would happen actually happened to Naaman. First, *'his flesh came again like unto the flesh of a little child'* – that is complete healing and restoration. *'And he was clean'* – that is total cleansing. If you, too, will put your trust in the blood of Jesus Christ today, you will find cleansing and complete healing.

Jesus Makes the Leper Whole

One of the most frequent miracles in the ministry of Jesus Christ when He was on earth was the cleansing

of lepers. This is very significant. He has come to
make every leper whole. A close study of the scripture where he cleansed the ten lepers shows that He
was fulfilling Old Testament scriptures about Him.
Let us take a look at it.

> And as he entered into a certain village, there met
> him ten men that were lepers, which stood afar off:
> And they lifted up their voices, and said, Jesus,
> Master, have mercy on us. And when he saw them,
> he said unto them, Go shew yourselves unto the
> priests. And it came to pass, that, as they went, they
> were cleansed. And one of them, when he saw that
> he was healed, turned back, and with a loud voice
> glorified God, and fell down on his face at his feet,
> giving him thanks: and he was a
> Samaritan.

Luke 17:12–16

*Men always think
they have better
ideas than God . . .
But the foolishness
of God is wiser
than men.*

As these ten lepers met Jesus,
they asked Him to show them
mercy. He spoke to them and,
by His word, made them whole.
Having been cleansed, He then
told them to go and present
themselves to the priest in order
to complete all the Old
Testament requirements. They believed, and the miracle took place. *'And it came to pass that, as they went,
they were cleansed'* (Luke 17:14).

Notice here that as they obeyed the words of Jesus
they were **cleansed**. But verse 15 is very significant:

> And one of them, when he saw that he was healed,
> turned back, and with a loud voice glorified God.

One of them saw that he was **healed**. That is it! Not only were they cleansed, they were healed, a complete fulfilment of the Old Testament shadow. We find this happening again and again throughout the life and ministry of our Lord Jesus Christ. Sometimes it was a single leper, sometimes there were more. But in each case He made them whole. He has not changed. He is '. . . *the same yesterday, and to day, and for ever*' (Hebrews 13:8). He is the perfect fulfilment of the Old Testament law.

Jesus shed His precious blood to cleanse us from the terrible leprosy of sin and to heal us of all the consequences of sin. If you believe, you can be made whole today.

If there is sin in your life, do not run away from God. Run to Him.

Right now, He does not want to judge you because of your sins no matter how terrible they are. It is only if you refuse to repent that judgment will certainly fall on you, sometime in the future. Whatever you are going through now is nothing to compare with the awful judgment that will fall on you if you choose not to repent.

Right now there is hope. The Son of man has come to seek and to save those who are lost in sin. He said clearly that He has not come to call the righteous to repentance but the unrighteous. If the leper of old had hope, then there is today, much more. No matter what your situation is, through the precious blood of Jesus, there is hope for you.

> *For the Son of man is come to seek and to save that which was lost.*
>
> Luke 19:10

8

Complete Redemption

Jesus . . . saith unto him, wilt thou be made whole?
John 5:6

The purpose of redemption is to make us whole –
spirit, soul and body, so that we may worship and
serve the Lord our God with our whole being. No
part of you is to remain under the dominion of the
devil. Complete redemption is God's plan for man. It
is what Jesus has secured for you by paying with His
precious blood.

Complete redemption touches every aspect of
your life.

Man, like God, is a tripartite being. You are a
whole person – spirit, soul and body. Some people
talk of man being just body and soul. They speak of
the inner man – soul, and the outer man – body. But
that is not accurate. The Bible makes it very clear that
man is a being of spirit, soul and body:

*And the very God of peace sanctify you wholly; and
I pray God your whole **spirit and soul and body**
be preserved blameless unto the coming of our Lord
Jesus Christ.*

I Thessalonians 5:23 (my emphasis)

I mentioned earlier that the blood of Jesus is the
means by which we are sanctified. This sanctification
is for your entire being – spirit, soul and body. God

wants to preserve you blameless for the glorious appearing of our Lord Jesus Christ. And that is what He paid for with His precious blood.

The Bible says we are to glorify God in our bodies and in our spirits which belong to God.

> *For ye are bought with a price: therefore glorify God in your body, and in your spirit, which are God's.*
> I Corinthians 6:20

Your body is no longer yours; your spirit is no longer yours. When Jesus paid the supreme price by shedding His blood on the cross, He paid to redeem your spirit, your soul and your body. And we are to glorify Him with our whole being.

You Are a Whole Man

You are not just a spirit. You are a human being. It is the combination of your spirit, your mind and your body that makes the complete you. Your spirit is your innermost being. It is by it you contact God. According to Watchman Nee, it carries the three faculties of intuition and worship. Because 'God is a Spirit', if you contact God at all it is through your spirit. You cannot contact Him with just your mind or body.

> *God is a Spirit: and they that worship him must worship him in spirit and in truth.*
> John 4:24

Your soul is that conscious part of you that carries the faculties of the intellect, the will and the emotions. It is with this you contact the intellectual world.

Your body is the outer shell that clothes the spirit and the soul. It has all the five senses of taste, touch, sight, smell and hearing, by which you contact the outside world.

When a man is sick in any of the three major aspects of his being, he is not whole. To be whole is to be sound in your spirit, your soul and your body. The blood of Jesus was shed to make you truly whole.

But we have always got things mixed up in this area.

A lot of people pay attention to the welfare of their bodies and utterly neglect their spirits. They pay a great deal of money to enjoy good health. They spend a fortune in order to look good, investing heavily in programmes and gadgets to shed excess weight and keep in good shape. These are not bad at all; but it must be realized that your spiritual welfare is more important, more critical, than your natural body.

Likewise, millions invest a fortune in developing the mind. They will pay any price to get a good education. This is good. But man is not just 'mind'. We possess a mind as one of our faculties. While struggling to develop your mind you must realize that for you to be truly whole you have to pay attention to the entire man – your spirit, your soul and your body. This will make you sound and well.

You are not just a spirit. You are a human being . . . Even though our bodies are mortal, while we are still in the flesh they are a crucial part of us. The body is the house for our spirit; it is the vehicle to convey whatever it is that God wants to accomplish through our spirits.

But here again is where many believers miss it.

They are born again and they pay quite a bit of attention to their spiritual development. They pray and fast. They spend a lot of time meditating in God's Word and they are always in the house of God to worship just as the Word of God commands. But they neglect their mental development and do not pay proper attention to the care of their bodies which are the temple of the Holy Spirit.

Even though our bodies are mortal, while we are still in the flesh they are a crucial part of us. The body is the house for our spirit; it is the vehicle to convey whatever it is that God wants to accomplish through our spirits by His Holy Spirit.

I have never seen the engine of a car running on the road all by itself without the body. No matter how strong, perfect or new the engine may be, it still needs the body to function. Your spirit is the engine. Your body is its house. You cannot function maximally without taking good care of your body. It is a vital part of your whole being. And Jesus Christ is Saviour of the body too. As a matter of fact, it is because He has redeemed your body by His precious blood that that body will be replaced by a glorious, immortal body at His return in the resurrection morning.

Beloved, you must recognize that God is interested in the whole you – spirit, soul and body and has paid to redeem the whole you – spirit, soul and body, so that you may love and serve the Lord your God with all your heart, with all your mind and with all your strength.

*Jesus said unto him, Thou shalt love the Lord thy God with **all thy heart**, and with **all thy soul**, and with **all thy mind**.*

Matthew 22:37 (my emphasis)

At the beginning of His ministry, Jesus announced His mission: redemption for man, complete deliverance that we may be made whole.

The Spirit of the Lord is upon me,
Because he hath anointed me to preach the gospel to
* the poor;*
He hath sent me to heal the brokenhearted, to preach
* deliverance to the captives,*
And recovering of sight to the blind,
To set at liberty them that are bruised.

Luke 4:18

While His ministry was in progress He made His mission clear, to redeem the whole you so that you may be free indeed.

If the Son therefore shall make you free, ye shall be free indeed.
John 8:36

And He succeeded in His task. He declared *'It is finished'* (John 19:30). The work of redemption is done and accomplished. Some people have argued that since resurrection was the climax of the redemption plan Jesus could not have said He had finished the work on the cross. But remember, Jesus did not raise Himself from the dead. He was raised by the power of God. As far as Jesus was concerned, what He needed to do had been done.

Beloved, you must recognize that God is interested in the whole you – spirit, soul and body and has paid to redeem the whole you – spirit, soul and body, so that you may love and serve the Lord your God with all your heart, with all your mind and with all your strength.

The blood had been shed. He had given His life. It was finished.

Complete redemption is available. However, it is your faith that makes it a reality. All things are ready. God is willing to bless, but it shall be to you according to your faith. This is important. The limiting factor is your faith. It is what you believe God for in His Word that He will give you.

I make bold to say to you that on the basis of what Jesus did for you on the cross of Calvary, complete redemption is available for you today. God the Father authenticated this when He raised his Son, Jesus, from the dead. The resurrection is an indication that the sacrifice of Jesus on the cross has met the claims of divine justice and was considered efficacious in red-eeming all mankind.

That God raised Jesus Christ from the dead is a proof that He is the redeemer of all mankind and what He did on the cross of Calvary fully paid for the sins of all human beings. However, this becomes a living reality only in those who put their trust in Jesus and the sacrifice of Calvary for their redemption.

Complete redemption is available. However, it is your faith that makes it a reality. All things are ready. God is willing to bless but it shall be to you according to your faith. This is important. The limiting factor is your faith. It is what you believe God for in His Word that He will give you. There are people who only know about salvation and forgiveness of sin. They clearly understand that aspect of our redemption and they believe it very firmly. While they are soundly born again, they may be very sick in their bodies or materially poor. They may even be living in fear, not knowing much about the believer's authority and dominion upon the earth. What is wrong? Does it mean all these other aspects of our redemption are no longer available? No, they are available. But these people have only understood and believed for salvation. According to their faith they got saved. But what they do not believe for, God is not going to give to them.

But beloved, go for complete redemption. Go for full salvation. What I am sharing with you now is the **full** gospel message. Your spirit, soul and body can be preserved blameless until the day of Christ. You can be free from sin. You can be free from sicknesses. You can be free from demonic afflictions. You can be free from poverty. You can reign in life with Christ Jesus and walk in complete dominion. This is what Jesus paid for on the cross of Calvary. Complete redemption is yours. Believe God for it today and let God perfect that which concerns you.

> *The LORD will perfect that which concerneth me:*
> *Thy mercy, O LORD, endureth for ever:*
> *Forsake not the works of thine own hands.*
>   Psalm 138:8

9

Five Points of Grace:
Complete Healing

The first edition of this book appeared under the title, *The Precious Blood of Jesus*, published in Nigeria in 1985. While working on its revision and subsequent expansion, the Lord brought clearly home to me some revelations about the blood of Jesus that I had never seen before. I want to share these for the edification of the body of Christ and to the glory of our God.

There were five major points from which our Lord Jesus shed His precious blood. In numerology, five is the figure for grace and victory. Jesus bled through His back, His head, His hands, His feet and His side. Each of these is very significant. Combining the five, we see the marvels of God's grace in providing complete redemption and absolute victory for us from all the vicious grips and devices of the devil. Our God is very precise, very exact. It really does matter how the blood was shed. There is a special message being communicated by each of the points from which Jesus shed His precious blood. Let us take a closer look at the crucifixion of Jesus Christ as narrated by John, the beloved.

By His Stripes

Then Pilate therefore took Jesus, and scourged him.
John 19:1

Pilate ordered Jesus to be scourged. According to Bible scholar J.F. Dakes, a scourge is not the same as a whip. It is a hydra-headed object with a thick handle and thirty-nine long branches with some dangerous objects like small stones or bones or metal fastened to the end of each. The prisoner is stripped, tied face down and the scourge is brutally applied to the bare flesh. As this hydra-headed scourge lands on the victim's body, it is pulled in such a way that the vicious objects at the end of each branch tear off some flesh and blood gushes out. That was the brutal treatment meted out to Jesus. He was so battered that He could not be easily recognized. His form, or visage, was marred beyond recognition.

As many were astonied at thee; his visage was so marred more than any man, and his form more than the sons of men.

Isaiah 52:14

This was the first major point through which the blood of Jesus flowed out.

Why was Jesus so brutalized? Why did He shed His blood through the body? The answer is clear in the Scriptures:

Surely he hath borne our griefs, and carried our sorrows: yet we did esteem him stricken, smitten of God, and afflicted. But he was wounded for our transgressions, he was bruised for our iniquities: the

*chastisement of our peace was upon him; and with
his stripes we are healed.*

                              Isaiah 53:4–5

We Are Healed

That Isaiah passage is one of the most significant
scriptures on redemption. It explains the divine
exchange that took place when Jesus took our place.

The Bible says, He bore *'our griefs'*, and He carried
'our sorrows'. I took time to check this up in a number
of translations of the Bible and I was astounded by
what I discovered. Actually, this was prompted by a
book I read in the early days of my Christian life entitled, *Christ The Healer* by Dr F. F. Bosworth. To make
this passage clearer, let us con-
sider a few translations quoted
below. In all these quotes, the
emphases are mine.

> *Our God is
> very precise, very
> exact. It really
> does matter
> how the blood
> was shed. There
> is a special
> message being
> communicated by
> each of the points
> from which Jesus
> shed His
> precious blood.*

*Yet it was our **pains** that he
bore, our sorrows that he carried.* (An American Translation)

Please take note of the word
'pains'. Pain is associated with
sickness, disease, affliction,
oppression and suffering. When
Jesus bore those pains on His
back and shed His blood, it was
your pains He was taking.

*Surely our **diseases** he did bear,
and our pains he carried.*
(A New Translation [Jewish])

Please note the word 'diseases'. Jesus bore those stripes and shed His precious blood, thereby taking away your diseases. He actually paid with His blood to make healing legally available to you; to take your diseases away, completely – all of them.

> *Yet surely our **sicknesses** he carried, and as for our pains he bare the burden of them.* (The Emphasized Bible.)

Did you notice the word 'sicknesses'? As Jesus was being scourged by the Roman soldiers, He was taking away all our sicknesses, making it possible for us to live in sound health. Your sickness can vanish right now, as you believe the efficacy of what Jesus did on Calvary's tree.

> *Yet it was our infirmities that he bore, our **sufferings** that he endured.* (New American Bible)

Two words are combined here – infirmities and sufferings. We **suffer** as a result of our **infirmities**. But when Jesus was scourged, he bore the infirmities that cause our sufferings, as well as the sufferings that result from our infirmities so that we may be free indeed.

Now put all of these together. Pain, disease, sickness, infirmity, suffering. The Bible makes it so plain that when Jesus was brutalized by the scourge, He bore all of these for us. You can be totally free from pain, disease, sickness, infirmity and suffering as you release your faith in Christ Jesus and claim your complete freedom.

Please note that the Bible passage under consideration begins with the word '*surely*'.

> *Surely he hath borne our griefs, and carried*

our sorrows.

Surely. Certainly. We are not guessing. We are stating
what actually happened. We are not speculating, we
are speaking the truth in love. There is nothing anyone can do against the truth but only for the truth. It
is a true saying that Jesus bore our sicknesses and our
pains on His body, thereby making healing available
for us:

> *. . . and with his stripes, we are
> healed.*
>
> Isaiah 53:5

**Now put all
of these together.
Pain, disease,
sickness,
infirmity, suffering.
The Bible makes it
so plain that when
Jesus was
brutalized by the
scourge, He bore all
of these for us.**

The Bible is very emphatic in its
declaration that with the stripes
of Jesus **we are healed.** You
need to identify with that in
order to experience it. If you
wholeheartedly identify with
the stripes that Jesus bore, then
you become one of those 'we'
that are healed.

Again, let us examine this
scripture from various translations:

. . . And by his stripes there is healing for us. (The
Emphasized Bible)

The blows that fell to him have brought us healing.
(Moffatt)

*By his stripes **we were healed.*** (New American
Bible, my emphasis)

And by his scourging we are healed. (New English
Bible)

He was lashed – and we were healed. (The Living
Bible)

These are the various insights God gave Bible scholars into what actually happened as Jesus was being
scourged. Those blows that fell on Him brought healing for us. The scourging He went through was to
make us whole. He was lashed and we were healed.
It has happened already: you only need to believe it
and it becomes a reality in your life.

I have just concluded a mass crusade in Ile-Ife, the
ancient city known as the cradle of the Yoruba race, in
the south-western part of Nigeria. The stadium was
packed every night for five days. On the third day, I
decided to allow a fairly long time to let people share
their testimonies of what God
had done in their lives. I was literally astonished. Sudden dis-
appearance of a tumour; cessa-
tion of blood flow in women;
sanity restored to people; deaf
and dumb spirits cast out. A lot
of astonishing testimonies of
God's healing power. How did
these miracles take place? I proclaimed boldly that through the
stripes Jesus bore, healing is
available for man. The people
believed it and God confirmed His Word.

> *I proclaimed boldly
> that through the
> stripes Jesus bore,
> healing is available
> for man. The people
> believed it and God
> confirmed His
> word.*

'*And with his stripes, we are healed.*'

Thank God Jesus was beaten. It was not pleasurable for Him. It was terrific pain for the sinless Son of
God. But as He was shedding His life blood through
those stripes, He was paying the price needed for
healing to become legally available to us as 'chil-

dren's bread' (Matthew 15:26).

Now I can reach out in faith and claim complete healing from any sickness, pain, disease or affliction, because Jesus paid the price to secure it for me. I do not have to beg God to heal me. He is my Father. I simply trust Him and believe what Jesus did to secure it for me. I am His child and not a beggar. A beggar begs and is uncertain of whether or not he will receive or be welcome at all. A child asks, confident that in the presence of his father he is not tolerated but celebrated, and knowing that all that the father has is his.

Beloved, Jesus bore all those pains for you. Not just for the fun of it, but that you may enjoy complete healing from head to toe. Do not let the enemy deceive you that it is not God's will that you be healed. That He allowed His Son to go through such agony for you is sufficient indication that your healing is His will. So much His will is it that He caused Jesus to pay for it in advance so you can simply receive it today. A close study of the Gospels reveal that our Lord Jesus spent a sizeable portion of His ministry on earth ministering to the sick. He took time to cast out demons and to raise the dead. If healing were not the will of God, Jesus would never do it. If healing were not the will of God, He would never have anointed His Son Jesus with the Holy Ghost and power so that He could heal

> *A beggar begs and is uncertain of whether or not he will receive or be welcome at all. A child asks, confident that in the presence of his father he is not tolerated but celebrated.*

all that were oppressed of the devil. But because healing was and is God's will, He did exactly that.

How God anointed Jesus of Nazareth with the Holy Ghost and with power: who went about doing good, and healing all that were oppressed of the devil; for God was with him.

Acts 10:38

Therefore beloved, believe God. It does not matter what your pain, or your previous experiences, or how long the problem has been there. It is finished. Do not wait until you see before you believe. Believe God. Take the first step of faith. Get out of your sickbed or situation of affliction and step into God's healing and liberty. As you step out in faith God will confirm His Word in your life and body. Your healing is already paid for. Go for it. Just believe God's Word, step out in faith, and you will see the glory of God.

Jesus saith unto her, Said I not unto thee, that, if thou wouldest believe, thou shouldest see the glory of God?

John 11:40

Matthew, the inspired writer of the Gospel named after him, said that the healing ministry of Jesus is a fulfilment of Isaiah's prophecy.

When the even was come, they brought unto him many that were possessed with devils: and he cast out the spirits with his word, and healed all that were sick: **that it might be fulfilled which was spoken by Esaias the prophet, saying, Himself took our infirmities, and bare our sicknesses.**

Matthew 8:16–17 (my emphasis)

He himself took our infirmities and bore our sicknesses. The healing ministry is still as effective today as it was when Jesus walked on the face of the earth. Jesus Christ is the same yesterday, and today, and for ever (Hebrews 13:8). But this becomes effective only when you believe it. It is effective in my life because I believe that Jesus took my infirmities and bore my sicknesses just as I believe Jesus took my sins on Himself on the cross of Calvary. You cannot be saved unless you believe Jesus took your sins on Himself and died in your place. Likewise, you cannot be healed unless you believe Jesus took your infirmities and sicknesses on His body on the tree. Believe it today and you will see that the Word of God is true.

Beloved, this is not a new theory. It is not 'New Age', it is New Testament! The early disciples believed so firmly that Jesus paid for the healing of our bodies that they simply commanded people to be healed in Jesus' name. And God honoured their faith. God honoured the blood of His Son Jesus, had regard for the stripes He bore for the healing of mankind, and established their faith by causing great multitudes to get healed. God still does the same today. I see this happen again and again in our mass crusades in Nigeria, Africa and indeed all over the world.

As a matter of fact, Peter, looking back at Calvary and the wounds Jesus bore for you spoke of your healing in the past tense. Settled already. Paid for in full. Readily available for immediate collection!

By whose stripes ye were healed.
                                    I Peter 2:24

Act on your faith, beloved, and God will honour His word in your life and situation.

Would you please say this prayer with me right now, in faith, trusting the Lord to effect your healing by His power, right away:

> **Father, I thank You, that Jesus Christ died for me. I thank You that He shed His precious blood for me. I thank You that He bore those stripes for me.**
>
> **Right now, I put my faith in Jesus Christ, His precious blood, and the stripes He bore. I claim my complete healing, right now, in the name of Jesus.**
>
> **Sickness *(call its name if you know it)* I rebuke you in the name of Jesus. I confront you with the blood of Jesus. I bind you and I cast you out of this body. By His stripes I am healed. By His stripes, I am made whole. It is well with me right now.**
>
> **Thank You Father. In Jesus' mighty name I pray.   Amen.**

Beloved, you are healed. God has honoured the blood of His Son in your life. You are made completely whole. Step out in faith and enjoy your miracle.

10

Five Points of Grace: Blessed Not Cursed

The second major point from which Jesus shed His precious blood for us is the head. As before, this is critical. There is a divine reason, a grand purpose for it. Let us look at it in the Scriptures.

The Crown of Thorns

And the soldiers platted a crown of thorns, and put it on his head, and they put on him a purple robe.
                                                                John 19:2

The Roman soldiers made a crown from thorns and pressed it on the head of Jesus, and blood flowed from His holy brow. Then one of the soldiers took the reed they had earlier placed in his hands and hit his head with it. And the blood flowed still more:

*Then the soldiers of the governor took Jesus into the common hall, and gathered unto him the whole band of soldiers. And they stripped him, and put on him a scarlet robe. And when they had platted a crown of thorns, **they put it upon his head**, and a reed in his right hand: and they bowed the knee before him, and mocked him, saying, Hail, King of the Jews! And they spit upon him, and took the reed, and*

*smote him on the head. And after that they had
mocked him, they took the robe off from him, and put
his own raiment on him, and led him away to cruci-
fy him.*

Matthew 27:27–31 (my emphasis)

While working on this book, the Holy Spirit
impressed in my heart that there is a deep spiritual
significance in Jesus shedding His blood through the
head. I began to pray, search the Scriptures, think and
meditate until I got a breakthrough on it.

When a blessing lands on someone, it falls on his
head. That is why the Patriachs of old laid their hands
on their children's heads to bless them and transfer
the covenant blessing. That is why in the New
Testament hands are laid on the head to bless, to heal,
to ordain and to consecrate a man to God. Your head
is the seat of your life, the centre of control. Whatever
falls on your head affects your entire life and being.
As a matter of fact in some primitive cultures, people
consider their head so sacred that they worship it.
They see whatever happens to their head as deter-
mining their fate in life.

A curse works in exactly the same way. When a
curse rests upon a man, it rests on his head and affects
every area of his life negatively, controlling and dom-
inating his entire life.

The Original Curse

When man fell in the beginning, God put a curse on
him. This has affected mankind down the ages. This
is what God said:

And unto Adam he said, Because thou hast heark-

ened unto the voice of thy wife, and hast eaten of the
tree, of which I commanded thee, saying, Thou shalt
not eat of it: **cursed is the ground for thy sake;** *in*
sorrow shalt thou eat of it all the days of thy life;
thorns also and thistles shall it bring forth to
thee; *and thou shalt eat the herb of the field.*
Genesis 3:17–18 (my emphases)

The curse landed on man's head, controlling his
entire life. Please note that the symbol of that curse is
thorns. *'Thorns also and thistles shall it bring forth to
thee.'* When we say a man's life is full of thorns we
mean it is full of hardship – frustrations, difficulties,
obstacles, defeats, sorrows and pressures of all kinds.
These have characterized man's life since the fall.

But while Jesus was paying the price for our
redemption, He took upon His head (the seat of life)
the symbol of man's curse, which is the thorn, and
shed His precious blood as the thorns pierced His
brow. He allowed the curse to fall upon Himself so
that He might lift, cancel, revoke, annul, make void,
any form of curse in your life for ever.

When He shed His precious blood through His
head He was paying the price to free you from the
curse for ever. The price is already paid. No matter
what curse you have been struggling against, Jesus
has already paid to free you from it. What He paid
for, you must have. No curse must have a hold or
effect upon your life any longer. The Bible makes it
clear that Christ has redeemed us from the curse of
the law:

*Christ hath redeemed us from the curse of the law,
being made a curse for us: for it is written, Cursed
is every one that hangeth on a tree: that the blessing*

> *of Abraham might come on the Gentiles through*
> *Jesus Christ; that we might receive the promise of*
> *the Spirit through faith.*
>
> Galatians 3:13–14

Study this scripture carefully and absorb the revelation it carries now to you:

- Christ has paid a price to redeem you from the curse of the law and every form of curse.
- He did this when He became a curse for you. He took your place. He wore the symbol of your curse and bore the actual curse itself that you may be free.
- Having abolished the curse, He now released upon your life the covenant blessings of Abraham.
- Now, in Christ Jesus you can be completely free from every curse.

You can be blessed in the morning, at noon, in the evening, at night. You can walk in the blessing of the Lord every day of your life. You can find yourself in a situation where every curse is gone, and the blessing of the Lord is upon your life. *'Ye are blessed of the LORD which made heaven and earth'* (Psalm 115:15).

Blessed or Cursed?

There are so many people in our generation who are struggling with one curse or another. There are negative spiritual forces at work, making people's lives miserable and full of woe. They go from one frustration to another. They move from debt further into debt. Their home life is never stable. They are far from prosperity and joy. They work so hard, toiling night and day. However, no matter how hard they try, things always end up in tragedy.

If you are in such a situation, you need to be delivered from the curse. The good news is, there is deliverance available to you through the precious blood of Jesus Christ.

> *The price is already paid. No matter what curse you have been struggling against, Jesus has already paid to free you from it.*

Dr Derek Prince, that renowned Bible teacher, has listed seven indications of a curse in his excellent work, *Blessing or Curse: You Can Choose*. According to him (and I perfectly agree because what he says lines up with God's Word), the following list is an indication that a curse is at work in the life of an individual:

1. Mental and/or emotional breakdown.
2. Repeated or chronic sicknesses (especially if hereditary).
3. Barrenness, a tendency to miscarry or related female problems.
4. Breakdown of marriage and family alienation.
5. Continuing financial insufficiency.
6. Being 'accident-prone.'
7. A history of suicides and unnatural or untimely deaths.

The presence of one or two of these in a man's life does not necessarily mean a curse is at work, but when there is a combination of many of these, then a curse is certainly at work.

If a curse alights upon an individual there must be

a reason for it. The Bible is very clear about this:

As the bird by wandering, as the swallow by flying,
So the curse causeless shall not come.

Proverbs 26:2

It could be an inherited curse that has been working in the family; it could be due to past sins or behaviour of the individual or it may be due to some demonic attacks. However, when a curse is at work in a man's life, the purpose is to fill that life with sorrow, frustration, defeat and suffering.

Ten Kinds of Curses

Sometime ago, I sat down to study the Scriptures on this subject of curses. What I discovered was astonishing. More people are operating under the influence of one curse or another than we imagine, even in the church.

But today, every curse shall be broken in your life.

There are **ten** different kinds of curse revealed in the Scriptures.

The curse of God

Yes, God curses when people violate His Word. That is what happened in Genesis chapter 3.

The curse of the LORD is in the house of the wicked:
but he blesseth the habitation of the just.

Proverbs 3:33

The curse of man

When a man who has lawful authority over you places a curse because you wronged him, it sticks and affects your life. Noah cursed Canaan and his descendants. Many children have been cursed by their parents.

For God commanded, saying, Honour thy father and mother: and, He that curseth father or mother, let him die the death.

Matthew 15:4

Self-inflicted curses

Some people make terrible pronouncements about themselves and heap awful curses upon themselves, sometimes in order to save their face or escape punishment. And the curses catch up with them later in life.

The curse of sowing and reaping

If you sow evil you reap evil. If you sow to the flesh you reap corruption. If you sow good you reap good. A lot of people are under a curse today which is a direct product of what they have done in the past.

The curse of the prophets

Beware of the prophets! When a man is genuinely anointed of the Holy Spirit, if you touch him you will pay the price! Gehazi lied to Elisha and he reaped leprosy for life.

He suffered no man to do them wrong:
Yea, he reproved kings for their sakes;
Saying, Touch not mine anointed,
And do my prophets no harm.

Psalm 105:14–15

The curse of the accursed

When you bring an accursed thing into your house or you associate with someone who is cursed or you live in a place where there is a curse, you partake of the curse. The anger of God against Israel in the days of Achan was not just because Achan stole, awful as that was, but because he stole 'the accursed thing'.

> *But the children of Israel committed a trespass in the*
> *accursed thing: for Achan, the son of Carmi, the son*
> *of Zabdi, the son of Zerah, of the tribe of Judah, took*
> *of the accursed thing: and the anger of the LORD was*
> *kindled against the children of Israel.*
>
> Joshua 7:1

Generational or inherited curses

A curse, like a blessing, does not die with the man.
When Abraham died, Isaac carried on the blessing of
the covenant. Likewise, when a wicked man who is
under the curse of the Lord dies, he transmits the
curse onto his children. As a matter of fact the children partake of the curse before the man dies. So
many people suffer terrible curses today not because
of what they have done, but because of their root and
origin.

> *Thou shalt not bow down thyself to them, nor serve*
> *them: for I the LORD thy God am a jealous God, vis-*
> *iting the iniquity of the fathers upon the children*
> *unto the third and fourth generation of them that*
> *hate me.*
>
> Exodus 20:5

The curse of unforgiveness

When a man lives in unforgiveness and bitterness, he
brings himself under a curse. Because you hold people's sins and offences against them, God holds your
sins and offences against you. Bitterness and unforgiveness are two very expensive commodities you
just cannot afford. They bring a curse faster than anything you know.

> *Follow peace with all men, and holiness, without*
> *which no man shall see the Lord: looking diligently*

*lest any man fail of the grace of God; lest any root of
bitterness springing up trouble you, and thereby
many be defiled.*

Hebrews 12:14–15

The curse of the law

When God's law is broken, a curse is automatically
released upon the man who breaks it. This kind of
curse is not removed except through thorough repentance and a complete turning to God in total obedience.

The curse of Satan

I put this last because it is the cheapest to handle.
Satan through his agents can put a curse on an individual who is outside Christ or has broken the hedge
of divine protection. Many people in our generation
suffer from this kind of curse. But if you are truly a
child of God and you are walking in complete obedience, under the cover of the blood of Jesus, the curse
of Satan cannot affect you a bit. As Balaam of old was
frustrated while trying to curse Israel, the enemy
shall be frustrated trying to curse you.

*How shall I curse, whom God hath not cursed?
Or how shall I defy, whom the LORD hath not defied.*

Numbers 23:8

I have gone to these lengths in trying to explain different curses, not to frighten you, but to expose the
devices of the enemy so you can deal with him effectively. In all these cases, identify what the problem in
your life is. In many cases you will have to engage
yourself in a comprehensive repentance that is thorough and genuine. You may have to restitute your
ways by throwing away the accursed thing, quitting

the accursed place, like Lot quit Sodom, or restoring a stolen good to the owner. You may have to meet with the person who was wronged and ask for his blessing. But in all cases, for the curse to be effectively destroyed, you have to turn to God wholeheartedly and apply the blood of Jesus Christ by faith.

Jesus Paid it All

When Jesus wore the crown of thorns, He took upon Himself your curse and made it possible for you to be free from every form of curse and enjoy the full blessings of God. However, this becomes real only after you put your faith in Him and the blood that He shed and claim your complete deliverance from every curse. You can enjoy that liberty today, if you will call upon the name of the Lord with all your heart:

> *And it shall come to pass, that whosoever shall call on the name of the LORD shall be delivered: for in mount Zion and in Jerusalem shall be deliverance, as the LORD hath said, and in the remnant whom the LORD shall call.*

> Joel 2:32

I heard someone preaching the other day, explaining that the black race was cursed. Taking his text from Genesis, he expounded how Noah cursed Canaan, his grandson, the son of Ham. He explained how Africa is the land of Ham or Mizraim and that the blacks were cursed and that is why negative things have happened to them for centuries.

I nodded my head and said, 'Well, that may be true, but it held up only until Calvary.' I am aware this is a controversial issue. Ham sinned against his father by seeing his nakedness and, rather than covering it, reporting it to his brethren. Noah cursed Canaan, Ham's son, not Ham himself. So Canaan was cursed not Ham. Anthropologically and from records of Scripture, Africa is the land of Ham. The Canaanites were the descendants of Canaan. They were the same people God ordered Israel to wipe out utterly and to take their land. Israel now occupies the land of Canaan. The Canaanites are gone from the face of the earth; but lots of people still think that Africa, the land of Ham, was cursed as a result of Noah's pronouncement. A close study of that scripture, however, shows that Noah cursed Canaan not Ham. When you really want to give a man terrible pain you afflict his son.

However, at Calvary, Jesus paid for it all and bore the symbol of every curse. He shed His precious blood to make void all curses and release divine blessings and grace. He has abolished all the handwriting of the ordinances that was against us, that was contrary to us, nailing it to His cross. This I know to be absolutely true according to the revelation of God's Word.

Now I am free from every curse through the blood of the Lamb of God. I am blessed, not cursed.

In Christ Jesus there is neither male nor female, neither black nor white, neither Jew nor Gentile, neither bond nor free. All who believe are truly one in Christ Jesus, they are the true seeds of Abraham. They are blessed with faithful Abraham. That is the Word of God:

> So then they which be of faith are blessed with faith-
> ful Abraham . . .
>   For ye are all the children of God by faith in Christ
> Jesus. For as many of you as have been baptized into

Christ have put on Christ. There is neither Jew nor Greek, there is neither bond nor free, there is neither male nor female: for ye are all one in Christ Jesus. And if ye be Christ's, then are ye Abraham's seed, and heirs according to the promise.

Galatians 3:9, 26–29

For he is not a Jew, which is one outwardly; neither is that circumcision, which is outward in the flesh: But he is a Jew, which is one inwardly; and circumcision is that of the heart, in the spirit, and not in the letter; whose praise is not of men, but of God.

Romans 2:28–29

This is not an anti-Semitic teaching. I believe the Jews are a race chosen by God to spread His love all over the earth. I believe Abraham was a Jew in the flesh. I believe Jesus Christ was a Jew in the flesh. I believe God still has an end-time plan for the Jews in the flesh, and that they are God's time-piece on the face of the earth today. But I also know that God has chosen them as a starting point to spread His love to all mankind. I know that in the fullness of time God will bring together all things as one in Christ, and that the spiritual identification with God through

At Calvary, Jesus paid for it all and bore the symbol of every curse. He shed His precious blood to make void all curses and release divine blessings and grace. He has abolished all the handwriting of the ordinances that was against us, that was contrary to us, nailing it to His cross. This I know to be absolutely true according to the revelation of God's Word.

Christ is superior to any other form of identification. We who are in Christ are the real Jew, not in the flesh but in the spirit. We are the true circumcision. This becomes ours through the new birth experience which is the gateway into God's blessing. It is compulsory for **anyone** who truly wants to inherit the Kingdom of God; Jew or Gentile, white or black.

> *Having made known unto us the mystery of his will, according to his good pleasure which he hath purposed in himself: That in the dispensation of the fulness of times he might gather together in one all things in Christ, both which are in heaven, and which are on earth; even in him.*
>
> Ephesians 1:9–10

When Jesus shed His precious blood, He broke down all the walls of partition and made it possible for all to be one.

> *Beloved, stand on redemption ground! Do not allow the devil to give you a 'curse-psychology'. If you are in Christ Jesus, no matter your race or the colour of your skin or your origin, you are blessed not cursed.*

> *Blotting out the handwriting of ordinances that was against us, which was contrary to us, and took it out of the way, nailing it to his cross.*
>
> Colossians 2:14

Stand Firm in Your Liberty

Beloved, stand on redemption ground! Do not allow the devil to give you a 'curse-psychology'. If you are in Christ Jesus, no matter your race or the colour of your skin or your origin, you are blessed not cursed. If the enemy brings negative events or occur-rences your way, do not accept them as normal or as products of a 'curse that must be'. Hold the blood of Jesus Christ against the adversary, cast out all his neg-ative stuff and go for your blessing. If in your life things are not working out well then you are missing it somewhere. Settle down and be true to God and to yourself. Think through the issue in the light of the Scriptures. Ask God to reveal it to you. Deal with the problem by faith and go for your blessing by the blood of the Lamb.

In Christ Jesus you are blessed not cursed!

Not only did Christ cancel the curse forever, but He made it possible for you to walk in the covenant blessing of Abraham. Part of this covenant blessing He released on you is a divine immunity from any curse the adversary may bring against you. So long as you are walking in obedience to God, you are blessed and you cannot be cursed.

Now, as a true Israel of God, while you are walking in fellow-ship with Him, there is no curse anyone can place on you that will work.

> *Surely there is no enchantment against Jacob,*
> *Neither is there any divination against Israel:*
> *According to this time it shall be said of Jacob and of Israel,*
> *What hath God wrought!*
> Numbers 23:23

Not only did Christ cancel the curse forever, but He made it possible for you to walk in the covenant blessing of Abraham.

There is no enchantment, divination, fortune-telling

or witchcraft practice that can affect you anymore. You are now completely covered by the blood of Jesus.

> For ye are dead, and your life is hid with Christ in God.

Colossians 3:3

If the enemy tries to put a curse on you while you are walking in obedience to God's Word, two things happen. First, the curse is turned to a blessing upon you. Secondly, the curse boomerangs back on the adversary. God has blessed you, hence no one can curse you and succeed.

You are dwelling in the secret place of the Most High, under the shadow of the Almighty where the devil can do you no harm.

> He that dwelleth in the secret
>   place of the most High
> Shall abide under the shadow of
>   the Almighty.
> I will say of the LORD, He is my
>   refuge and my fortress:
> My God; in him will I trust.

Psalm 91:1–2

No weapon that is formed against you shall prosper and every mouth that the devil uses against you in judgment you will condemn by the blood of Jesus.

> In righteousness shalt thou be established: thou shalt be far from oppression; for thou shalt not fear: and from terror; for it shall not come near thee . . . No weapon that is formed against thee shall prosper; and every tongue that shall rise against thee in judgment thou shalt condemn. This is the heritage of the servants of the LORD, and their righteousness is of

me, saith the LORD.

Isaiah 54:14,17

If the enemy tries to put a curse on you while you are walking in obedience to God's Word, two things happen. First, the curse is turned to a blessing upon you. Secondly, the curse boomerangs back on the adversary. God has blessed you, hence no one can curse you and succeed. All because you put your faith in the blood that Jesus Christ shed for you.

How shall I curse, whom God hath not cursed?
Or how shall I defy, whom the LORD hath not
  defied? . . .
Behold, I have received commandment to bless:
And he hath blessed; and I cannot reverse it.

Numbers 23:8,20

In Christ you become a seed of Abraham by faith. And you are entitled to all the blessings of Abraham. All because of the blood of Jesus Christ, the Lamb of God.

And I will make of thee a great nation, and I will
bless thee, and make thy name great; and thou shalt
be a blessing.

Genesis 12:2

Rejoice, beloved, if you are in Christ Jesus. He has worn the symbol of your curse on His head. He gave His life blood to free you from all curses. You are the blessed of the Lord Most High.

Would you please pray this prayer on the next page with me, releasing yourself from every curse, commanding the blessing of the Lord upon your life:

Father, I thank You that the blood of Jesus Christ was shed for me. I thank You that He wore the crown of thorns on my behalf in order to lift every curse from my life.

Father, I sincerely repent of all my past sin, idolatry, immorality, unfaithfulness, that might have brought a curse upon my life. Right now, I plead the blood of Jesus upon my life. I cancel every curse, whether inherited, generational, ancestral, self-induced or demonically orchestrated. I void every curse. I revoke every negative covenant and agreement that has been working against me.

I wholeheartedly dedicate myself to Jesus, and to my Father God, to do Your will and walk in Your Word. I hereby release upon my life the covenant blessing of Abraham in every form. I am blessed in every area of my life. In Jesus' mighty name I pray.

Amen.

11

Five Points of Grace:
Abundant Life Released

Now came the crucifixion. After they scourged Him and put on Him the crown of thorns, Jesus was brought to a place called Golgotha and there they crucified Him:

> *Then delivered he him therefore unto them to be crucified. And they took Jesus, and led him away. And he bearing his cross went forth into a place called the place of a skull, which is called in the Hebrew Golgotha: where they crucified him, and two other with him, on either side one, and Jesus in the midst.*
> John 19:16–18

In crucifying Jesus they stretched His hands and nailed them to the cross. His blood flowed freely, with Him bearing excruciating pain. This was the third major point from which Jesus our Lord shed His precious blood.

His Hands Were Pierced

Why did He shed His blood through His hands?

Your hands are the symbol of your economic capability and strength. Your hands are used to labour and to gather wealth. You receive and give money with your hands. The Bible always talks of **'the work of your hands'** or **'that which you set your hands upon to do'** (Deuteronomy 28:8,12).

Let us look at some scriptures to explain these points clearly.

When Jacob was asking his children to go back again to Egypt to purchase food for the family, this is what he said:

> *And take double money in your hand; and the money that was brought again in the mouth of your sacks, carry it again **in your hand**; peradventure it was an oversight.*

> Genesis 43:12 (my emphasis)

You handle money with your hands. Your hands have to do with your prosperity. This is why a man who is lazy or idle shall come to poverty; but the diligent shall be made rich.

To further confirm that your hands have a lot to do with your economic activities, read what Moses said when speaking to Israel:

> *And there ye shall eat before the LORD your God, and ye shall rejoice in all that ye put your hand unto, ye and your households, wherein the LORD thy God hath blessed thee.*

> Deuteronomy 12:7

God wants to bless the work of your hands and prosper you abundantly in all that you set out to do. This is made clear in this covenant scripture given to Israel as well as to all who believe and trust God.

> *The LORD shall command the blessing upon thee in thy storehouses, and in all that thou settest thine hand unto; and he shall bless thee in the land which*

*the LORD thy God giveth thee . . . The LORD shall
open unto thee his good treasure, the heaven to give
the rain unto thy land in his season, and to bless all
the work of thine hand: and thou shalt lend unto
many nations, and thou shalt not borrow.*

Deuteronomy 28:8,12

One crucial area where the curse that came in
the fall affected man was his economy. Prior to
the fall man was living in God's abundance. All
he needed was freely available in the garden.
He did not need to sweat in
order to eat. Abundance was
at his finger tips. As a matter
of fact, God provided the
garden of abundance before
He made man. Eden means
abundance; pleasure; paradise; bliss; or delight. At the
fall, man was driven out of
Eden, from thenceforth to
live 'out of the sweat' of his
face. Prior to the fall, his land
yielded   superabundantly.
Now, following the fall, the
land 'shall no longer yield its
strength'. Poverty, hardship,
insufficiency and debt were
direct products of the curse.
The work of man's hands
was cursed and his economic capability diminished.
Poverty now replaced abundance.

> *Your hands are
> the symbol of
> your economic
> capability and
> strength. Your
> hands are used to
> labour and to
> gather wealth. You
> receive and give
> money with your
> hands. The Bible
> always talks of
> 'the work of your
> hands' or 'that
> which you set your
> hands upon to do'.*

A closer look at God's pronouncement on man

after the fall shows that man's economy and prosperity was terribly affected by the fall:

> *And unto Adam [God] said, Because thou hast hearkened unto the voice of thy wife, and hast eaten of the tree, of which I commanded thee, saying, Thou shalt not eat of it: cursed is the ground for thy sake; in sorrow shalt thou eat of it all the days of thy life; thorns also and thistles shall it bring forth to thee; and thou shalt eat the herb of the field; in the sweat of thy face shalt thou eat bread, till thou return unto the ground; for out of it wast thou taken: for dust thou art, and unto dust shalt thou return.*
>
> Genesis 3:17–19

There is death at last when man returns to the dust from which he was taken. But before then, the ground is cursed. There shall be hardship, sorrow, reduced productivity, sweating to eat and a hard struggle for survival. Poverty became a major consequence of the fall of man.

Poverty Is an Issue

Recently, I was reading a book on world missions. The sorry state of our world was graphically portrayed on the pages of that book and gripping statistics of man's sufferings were laid out clearly.

The contents of the book further underscored the fact that poverty is a major cause of human suffering and agony in this world. Let me quote a portion for you:

> I am sad to know that 40,000 children die due to hunger. God cannot be happy to look down from his throne in heaven to see that 750 mil-

lion sleep every night with an empty stomach; 100 million sleep each night without a roof over them.

Do you know that 900 million people sleep in shanties of cardboard or scrap tin each night? Does it touch your heart that millions live on garbage dumps, with no sanitation and die cheaply due to lack of simple drugs? There are 20 million street kids in South American cities alone. And I cannot bear the thought that 100,000 die each day who never heard the name of Christ. They die as if the Lord had not suffered for them and taken their place. While they drop dead like pawpaw and sink to the bottomless pit, churches are busy spending money on breath-taking buildings and programs that only amount to showbiz. Meanwhile, 2.5 billion people are still waiting worldwide to hear the Gospel, mainly in countries that lie between latitudes 10 and 40 degrees known as 10/40 window.*

If poverty was a major issue at the fall, and if poverty is still a major problem of our world now, then a redemption that does not address poverty is incomplete and inadequate.

But when Jesus stretched out His hands and allowed the nails to pierce Him, He was paying the price to cancel poverty and release abundance. He opened those same hands that flung stars into space and allowed them to be pierced by cruel nails. He became poor for your sake so that you, through His poverty, may be rich.

---

* Emmanuel Falola, *Let me Run: A Call to Missions*, pp 10–11.

For ye know the grace of our Lord Jesus Christ, that, though he was rich, yet for your sakes he became poor, that ye through his poverty might be rich.

II Corinthians 8:9

Jesus was rich in all ways, but He became poor to identify with our poverty. The result? *'That ye through his poverty might be rich.'*

The Bible is not talking of 'spiritual poverty' here as some will want us to believe. Jesus was never at any time spiritually poor. But He tasted physical poverty in order to cancel poverty. The abundant life that Jesus has brought for us includes financial and material prosperity:

The thief cometh not, but for to steal, and to kill, and to destroy: I am come that they might have life, and that they might have it more abundantly.

John 10:10

By shedding that precious blood through His hands, Jesus released the covenant blessing of wealth upon your hands – the power to get and create wealth. Jesus paid for it with his precious blood. God is doing that in order to establish His covenant upon the earth:

But thou shalt remember the LORD thy God: for it is he that giveth thee power to get wealth, that he may establish his covenant which he sware unto thy fathers, as it is this day.

Deuteronomy 8:18

A friend in Europe raised an objection to a portion of my book dealing with prosperity as God's will for us.

'We do not need this health and wealth stuff,' he said. 'God is not particular about that; he just wants people saved, to become true disciples and make it to heaven.'

I looked at him. He had a flourishing business. He lives in a large country house with a very spacious garden, lawns well mowed. He drives a good car – a BMW. His wife is a doctor and drives a beautiful Vauxhall car. They are quite comfortable. I am happy that this family is genuinely saved and they are not in any way materialistic. However, the fact is: they are quite comfortable. They have never tasted the pangs of poverty and homelessness, hence, they do not know by experience what it is to be liberated from poverty. They are already enjoying abundant life, because of the gospel.

If poverty was a major issue at the fall, and if poverty is still a major problem of our world, then a redemption that does not address poverty is incomplete and inadequate.

The foundation for the affluent lifestyle of the western world today was laid with the gospel message that was preached centuries ago. Let us preach the complete message of redemption to the poor. God does not want man poor. He wants to bless and prosper the work of his hands. Jesus shed His precious blood to redeem us from every curse of the law, including poverty. You can be free from it for ever and enjoy God's abundance all your days.

Make no mistake about it, one of the areas where the enemy can hold you to ransom and frustrate your life is in finances. There are many more people in prison now for money-related offences than for all other offences put together. And so many are in terrible bondage financially. Debt. Unemployment.

Mortgages. Bank overdrafts. Credit card payments. Unpaid bills. Unredeemed pledges and vows. So many know nothing about financial freedom. They are getting deeper into debt by the day.

Please understand this, beloved: there are demons of poverty Satan has sent to attack our generation. Individuals, families, homes, institutions, companies and entire nations are under their attack. Even churches and Christian ministries are not spared. There are demons that hold people down in financial bondage, lack and insufficiency, whilst making people think that money matters are not spiritual. They lie to people that God does not give it much attention and they have to struggle on their own.

The Spiritual Root

I have come to discover that poverty and prosperity have spiritual roots and connections.

All through the Scriptures, poverty is related to disobedience, rebelliousness and sin, while prosperity is associated with complete obedience to God. Hear what the Bible says:

> *If ye be willing and obedient, ye shall eat the good of the land.*
>
> Isaiah 1:19

> *If they obey and serve him,*
> *They shall spend their days in prosperity,*
> *And their years in pleasures.*
>
> Job 36:11

> *Bring ye all the tithes into the storehouse, that there may be meat in mine house, and prove me now herewith, saith the LORD of hosts, if I will not open you*

the windows of heaven, and pour you out a blessing,
that there shall not be room enough to receive it.

Malachi 3:10

Whenever God's people walk in obedience and righteousness, they lay a solid foundation for prosperity and abundance. When they lapse into disobedience, rebelliousness and sin, they come under the curse of poverty.

God has put abundance into every portion of the earth. But it is obedience to His Word that releases it.

Africa is suffering today, not because the continent is poor, but as a result of centuries of idolatry, superstition and witchcraft. Right now we are clearing up the continent by the Word of God and the blood of the Lamb. Just watch out and see what happens. There shall be abundance and prosperity in Africa and it shall affect the entire world.

Observe what is happening to Russia today. They had the gospel, the foundation was laid for years of prosperity. Then came Communism and ungodliness. They forsook God and the foundation for true prosperity was destroyed. Now they are in the woods politically and economically and there is no end in sight. Until they turn fully to the Lord there can be no restoration. The same is true for individuals, for families, for cities and for nations. God gives power to get wealth when there is obedience to His Word.

. . . for it is he that giveth thee power to get wealth,
that he may establish his covenant which he sware
unto thy fathers, as it is this day.

Deuteronomy 8:18b

Beloved, poverty is an enemy. Jesus conquered it on the cross by allowing His hands to be pierced to free

you from its grips. You can be free indeed today. You
can move from minus to plus, from zero to surplus. You can handle abundance. You can lay hold of what Jesus has done. Your hands can carry a divine touch such that all that you lay those hands on shall flourish.

*Whenever God's
people walk in
obedience and
righteousness,
they lay a solid
foundation for
prosperity and
abundance.*

His hands were pierced that your hands may be blessed. Believe what He did for you and let Heaven release abundance on your hands.

*The LORD shall command the
blessing upon thee in thy storehouses, and in all that
thou settest thine hand unto; and he shall bless thee
in the land which the LORD thy God giveth thee . . .*
**The LORD shall open unto thee his good treas-
ure, the heaven to give the rain unto thy land in
his season, and to bless all the work of thine
hand:** *and thou shalt lend unto many nations, and
thou shalt not borrow.*

Deuteronomy 28:8,12 (my emphasis)

Would you please pray this prayer with me. Stretch
open your palms as you pray and prophesy.

**Father, in the name of Jesus Christ, I thank You
that Jesus died to redeem me from poverty and lack.
His hands were pierced that my hands may be
blessed. Right now, I reject every form of lack and
poverty in my life in the name of Jesus Christ. I
reject every form of insufficiency and want. You**

have promised to supply all my need according to your riches in glory.

Right now, I command abundance and prosperity upon these hands in the name of Jesus Christ. I release upon these hands the covenant blessing of Abraham. From today, everything I touch with these hands shall be blessed according to the Word of God.

Thank You Father, I know Your Word works for me. In Jesus' mighty name. Amen.

12

Five Points of Grace:
Dominion Restored

As we continue in our close examination of the crucifixion of our Lord Jesus, you will discover that every point from which He shed His blood is eternally significant.

Next to be pierced were His feet; as they were nailed to the cross, His precious blood flowed freely. Every drop of His blood that was shed was payment for us. He gave His life blood and redeemed us from the fall with its awful consequences. There is no way we can talk of our redemption and not refer to the fall of man. It was the fall that made redemption necessary. Redemption was to counter and nullify the effects of the fall, and unfold God's eternal plan for blessing mankind.

At the fall there was an extremely significant prophecy, a word God spoke while putting a curse on the serpent. It shows us the rainbow through the rain. God remembered and promised mercy in the time of extreme wrath:

And the LORD God said unto the serpent, Because thou hast done this, thou art cursed above all cattle, and above every beast of the field; upon thy belly shalt thou go, and dust shalt thou eat all the days of

thy life: And I will put enmity between thee and the
woman, and between thy seed and her seed; it shall
bruise thy head, and thou shalt bruise his heel.

Genesis 3:14–15

We know the old serpent is the devil, Satan, the
deceiver. We know Jesus is the promised seed of the
woman. From the time God made that pronouncement, Satan went looking for the seed of the woman.
He thought it was Abel, hence, he got Abel killed. He
thought it was Moses and stirred Pharaoh to do his
best to kill all the male children. When Jesus was born
Satan incited Herod to kill all male children aged two
years and below. He was searching for the woman's
seed. In all these he missed it terribly. God has always
been ahead of the adversary!

But at the crucifixion, Jesus – the actual seed of the
woman – allowed his feet to be bruised, thereby fulfilling a prophetic word pronounced four thousand
years earlier. And the devil really bruised His heel.
The scar is there to be seen, even right now as Jesus
sits on the throne – the scar of God's eternal love for
mankind.

By letting His heel be bruised, Jesus paid the price
and fulfilled that prophecy. It is now certain that
Satan's head is crushed in exchange. Indeed Jesus
smashed Satan's head on the cross. The Bible has this
to say about it.

And having spoiled principalities and powers, he
made a shew of them openly, triumphing over them
in it.

Colossians 2:15

Forasmuch then as the children are partakers of flesh
and blood, he also himself likewise took part of the

same; that through death he might destroy him that
had the power of death, that is, the devil; and deliv-
er them who through fear of death were all their life-
time subject to bondage.

Hebrews 2:14–15

You can see that Jesus spoilt principalities and powers of darkness. He made a show of them openly. He
triumphed over them in absolute victory.

Through His death He destroyed or vanquished
the one who had the power of death, that is the devil.
He conquered all the powers of darkness and
obtained absolute dominion over them.

Now, Jesus did not need to conquer the devil for
Himself. He had never at any time been under the
dominion of the devil. Never. He is God from all
eternity. But mankind had been under the dominion
of Satan right from the fall. If He was going to liber-
ate us, He needed to identify Himself with us in our
state of bondage. That is why, according to the will of
the Father, He submitted Himself in death to the
powers of darkness that they might triumph for a
short time, in order that He might break our chains of
slavery forever and restore dominion to man.

But that was not the end of the story. Jesus allowed
His feet to be bruised to make it possible for you to
bruise the head of the serpent all your life, and walk
in dominion on earth. This actually was the original
plan of God for man at creation.

Hear what God said:

And God said, Let us make man in our image, after
our likeness: and let them have dominion over the
fish of the sea, and over the fowl of the air, and over
the cattle, and over all the earth, and over every

creeping thing that creepeth upon the earth. So God
created man in his own image, in the image of God
created he him; male and female created he them.

Genesis 1:26–27

The crown of dominion fell from man's head at the
fall. But Jesus put it right back in place after His death
and glorious resurrection. The prince of this world
did not understand the wisdom of God, that through
His death Jesus was going to get hold of the enemy
and free humanity by destroying the yoke of
bondage, lifting man back to the position of dominion. That is exactly what happened. This makes Jesus'
prophecy in Luke a legal reality.

And he said unto them, I beheld Satan as lightning
fall from heaven. Behold, I give unto you power to
tread on serpents and scorpions, and over all the
power of the enemy: and nothing shall by any means
hurt you.

Luke 10:18–19

Walking upon serpents and
scorpions and over all the powers of the enemy is now your
birthright – secured with the
precious blood of Jesus Christ.

Jesus' feet were bruised in
order to put Satan and his
hosts under your feet forever.
Like the first Adam you can
now walk in dominion upon
the earth and make the devil
kiss the dust. You are to reign
in Christ Jesus and enjoy complete victory.

Jesus allowed
His feet to be
bruised to make it
possible for you to
bruise the head of
the serpent all your
life, and walk
in dominion on
the earth.

For if by one man's offence death reigned by one;
much more they which receive abundance of grace
and of the gift of righteousness shall reign in life by
one, Jesus Christ.

Romans 5:17

This is not to say that the enemy will not fight or resist you, but absolute victory is certain. It was secured for you with the precious blood of Jesus.

> *The crown of dominion fell from man's head at the fall. But Jesus put it right back in place after His death and glorious resurrection.*

Now beloved, you are no longer supposed to be afraid of the adversary. He is completely under your feet. You are not to be scared of witches and wizards and the powers of darkness – not one bit. If you are in Christ Jesus, covered by His precious blood, you have absolute victory over them all. They cannot hinder you from getting to God's goal and purpose for your life. Arise and tread. The enemy is already under your feet.

The Joshua Generation

I believe with all my heart that we are the Joshua generation – the generation that will subdue the enemies, possess the land and bring back Christ our King to reign upon the earth. Yes we are.

There is a great difference between Moses and Joshua. Moses was a pioneer, but he did not finish the job. He was a liberator, but not a deliverer. He took the people out of Egypt, but did not succeed in taking them into the promised land. He himself did not even enter before God took him. But Joshua succeeded where Moses failed. He took the people right into the promised land.

When Joshua got to the promised land, he began to fight, defeating the enemies in the name of the Lord. At one of those battles, great miracles happened. The sun stood still for a whole day; likewise the moon. Then God rained hailstones from heaven, fighting for Joshua so that the men killed by the hailstones were many more than those killed by Joshua and his men. Talk of supernatural assistance in spiritual warfare through mighty signs, wonders, miracles and angelic interventions – we shall have them again in our days. These are the days when decisive battles must be fought and won for the Lord, and precious souls in the grip of Satan liberated, set free and brought into God's kingdom.

> *I believe with all my heart that we are the Joshua generation – the generation that will subdue the enemies, possess the land and bring back Christ our King to reign upon the earth. Yes we are.*

Five kings came together as a confederate against Joshua. They were the allied forces against God's people. Joshua defeated them and the kings fled and hid themselves in a cave. Joshua then ordered the cave sealed until the battle was over. After the enemies were routed, their kings were brought out before Joshua and all the elders of Israel. Joshua ordered them to lie down and then he asked all the elders of Israel to put their feet on the necks of these adversaries of the Lord. Then came the word of prophecy by Joshua.

*And it came to pass, when they brought out those kings unto Joshua, that Joshua called for all the men of Israel, and said unto the captains of the men of war which went with him, Come near, put your feet upon the necks of these kings. And they came near, **and put their feet upon the necks of them**. And Joshua said unto them, Fear not, nor be dismayed, be strong and of good courage: for thus shall the LORD do to all your enemies against whom ye fight.*

Joshua 10:24–25 (my emphasis)

The Lord is putting your feet on the necks of your adversaries right now, beloved. The victory was secured for you with the precious blood of Jesus Christ. His feet were bruised that your feet may be permanently on the adversaries' necks. You shall yet reign and triumph in the midst of your foes. All the 'Egyptians' you see now, you shall never see again. You have victory now, through the precious blood of Jesus.

And the God of peace shall bruise Satan under your feet shortly.
The grace of our Lord Jesus Christ be with you. Amen.

Romans 16:20

13

Five Points of Grace:
The Fountain of Life

Then came the soldiers, and brake the legs of the
first, and of the other which was crucified with
him. But when they came to Jesus, and saw that
he was dead already, they brake not his legs: but
one of the soldiers with a spear pierced his side,
and forthwith came there out blood and water.
And he that saw it bare record, and his record
is true: and he knoweth that he saith true,
that ye might believe.
John 19:32–35

The fifth major point from which Jesus shed His precious blood was His side. This was a clear fulfilment of an Old Testament prophecy, given by Zechariah long before Jesus was born: *'They shall look on him whom they pierced'* (John 19:37; Zechariah 12:10).

The Jewish authorities did not want the body of Jesus and those of the two thieves that were crucified with Him to hang on the cross for too long, because of their preparation for the high Sabbath. So the soldiers came to break their legs so that they might die quickly. (They used their legs to support the body to be able to breath.) They broke the legs of the two thieves, but on getting to Jesus they discovered He was dead already. Hence his bones were not broken, fulfilling another scripture, *'A bone of him shall not be broken'* (John 19:36; Exodus 12:46).

Then one of the soldiers plunged a spear into Jesus' side. Doing this he opened up a fountain, and blood and water gushed out. The Bible speaks of this:

> *In that day there shall be a fountain opened to the house of David and to the inhabitants of Jerusalem for sin and for uncleanness.*
>
> Zechariah 13:1

That is God's fountain of life – opened at Emmanuel's side – for sin and for uncleanness. That is the fountain the entire race of mankind had been waiting for in order to be free from sin and uncleanness. That is God's fountain of grace. That is God's fountain of compassion and mercy.

Now you can be completely free from sin in all its ramifications. Just one drop of that precious blood and your sins are gone for ever. It does not really matter the magnitude of the sins or the extent of the damage they have done to you. All you need do is come to the fountain and you are free for ever.

Holiness Is Imperative

As you must have discovered from the beginning of this book, sin in the life of man is the major issue that God has to deal with. When a man is free from sin, he is free indeed. When a man is not yet free from sin, he is not free at all.

Now you have to be free from sin:

- If you want to make it to heaven.

- If you want to see God.
- If you want to be a vessel of honour in the hands of God.
- If you want to enjoy complete dominion over the devil and his hosts.
- If you want to enjoy peace with God.
- If you want to enjoy all the blessings of redemption that Jesus Christ purchased for us at Calvary.
- If you want to be under the mighty anointing of the Holy Spirit.

Make up your mind, beloved, there can be no compromise with sin if you really want to enjoy God. Like John Wesley of old put it, it is either holiness or hell.

> *Follow peace with all men, and holiness, without which no man shall see the Lord.*
>
> Hebrews 12:14

> *Blessed are the pure in heart: for they shall see God.*
> Matthew 5:8

Entire Sanctification

God is so holy that if we are to fellowship with Him at all, we must be purified from all sin. The Bible makes it very clear that the perfect will of God for us is entire sanctification – that *'Having therefore these promises, dearly beloved, let us cleanse ourselves from all filthiness of the flesh and spirit, perfecting holiness in the fear of God'* (II Corinthians 7:1). To compromise this is to compromise your peace with God and your eternal destiny. God's perfect will is that your entire spirit, soul and body be preserved blameless until the coming of our Lord Jesus Christ.

And the very God of peace sanctify you wholly; and I pray God your whole spirit and soul and body be preserved blameless unto the coming of our Lord Jesus Christ.

1 Thessalonians 5:23

> *Now you can be completely free from sin in all its ramifications. Just one drop of that precious blood and your sins are gone for ever. It does not really matter the magnitude of the sins or the extent of the damage they have done to you.*

Please note from the scripture above that blamelessness is God's will for us. And this affects

- your spirit
- your soul
- your body.

Now, there is no single man who has walked this earth and been absolutely blameless from birth till death. Every man has a record of sin, except Jesus – the Holy One of God. This is where the blood of Jesus Christ comes in. That precious blood was shed to cleanse us from every iniquity and to make us blameless before God. Our God has promised us entire sanctification and cleansing from every sin. The word of God declares that He who has promised is faithful: He will do it. Therefore, trust Him to purify your spirit, soul and body from every defilement and sin today.

Faithful is he that calleth you, who also will do it.

1 Thessalonians 5:24

Agents of Sanctification

There are specific means by which a man can experience cleansing from the defilment of the world. It is possible for you to live a holy, clean life in this world, according to the will of the Father.

Repentance is the first step towards entire sanctifcation. The key word in repentance is change! There must be a change of attitude towards sin . . . about that sin in your life. You must hate it. You must loathe it. You must be willing to confess it to God, claiming complete cleansing by His mercies. You must change from sin and turn your entire life to God.

> Repent ye therefore, and be converted, that your sins may be blotted out, when the times of refreshing shall come from the presence of the Lord; and he shall send Jesus Christ, which before was preached unto you: whom the heaven must receive until the times of restitution of all things, which God hath spoken by the mouth of all his holy prophets since the world began.
>
> Acts 3:19–21

Sanctification also comes by prayer. Calling upon the Lord in sincerity and truth, asking Him to create in you a clean heart and a right spirit.

> Hide thy face from my sins,
> And blot out all mine iniquities.
> Create in me a clean heart, O God;
> And renew a right spirit within me.
> Cast me not away from thy presence;
> And take not thy holy spirit from me.
>
> Psalm 51:9–11

The Word of God is a mighty agent of entire sanctification. Jesus said to His disciples, 'Now ye are *clean through the word which I have spoken unto you'* (John 15:3). The Bible makes it clear that God cleanses His church by the washing through the Word of God. When you receive the engrafted Word of God into your spirit, you are truly, truly cleansed. *'Sanctify them through thy truth: thy word is truth'* (John 17:17)

Faith is a means of sanctification. You have to believe God that it is possible to be cleansed and free from sin. You have to receive God's Word by faith and allow it to purify your heart. Faith in God'sWword brings cleansing from the defilement of sin. God told Paul He was sending him to the Gentiles to proclaim the Good News to them, that they might become *'sanctified by faith'* (Acts 26:18).

The Holy Spirit also has a powerful sanctifying ministry to anyone who opens his or her heart to Him. He is holy. He makes us holy. He is God's purifying fire that comes to burn off all the chaff of ungodliness and uncleanness out of our hearts. When a heart is truly open to this sanctifying fire of the Holy Spirit, it is purified indeed.

The apostle Paul talks of how his life was full of sin and wickedness in the past. However, it changed when the Holy Spirit came upon him in His sanctifying power. May you experience the cleansing power of the Spirit of the living God today.

For we ourselves also were sometimes foolish, disobedient, deceived, serving divers lusts and pleasures, living in malice and envy, hateful, and hating one another. But after that the kindness and love of God our Saviour toward man appeared, not by works of righteousness which we have done, but according to his mercy he saved us, by the washing of regeneration, and renewing of the Holy Ghost;

which he shed on us abundantly through Jesus Christ our Saviour.

Titus 3:3–6

Sanctification comes by the blood of the Lamb of God. This has been strongly emphasised in this book. As the blood of the atoning bird cleansed the leper of the Old Testament of his leprosy, the blood of Jesus cleanses anyone who comes to it, and makes him whiter than snow. Without the blood of Jesus Christ, entire sanctification is completely impossible.

Free Indeed

Through the blood of Jesus you can be free from the guilt of sin and its awful consequent judgment. You know, when you sin, first and foremost you wrong God, you break His holy law, you hurt Him. You are guilty and consequently you should be judged and punished. The wages of sin is death (Romans 6:23).

But when you genuinely repent of your sins and take advantage of that fountain opened at Jesus' side from where His blood flowed, God is appeased. Rather than judgment, He releases mercy, acquits you of your guilt and commutes the deserved punishment. Because of His mercies released through the blood of Jesus, you are not given the rightful and just punishment that you deserved. Thank God for the blood of Jesus. By His blood your guilt is removed. Your sentence is commuted. Divine mercy is shown to you. Alleluia!

This is not all. Sin is the most damaging thing that can ever happen to man. By it you are defiled and rendered unclean. You are weakened spiritually and left open to satanic attacks. But when you take advantage of the blood of Jesus it deals decisively with the pains of sin. The condemnation; the guilty conscience; the defilement; the weakening of your spiritual man; the pollution of your faculties; all these are wiped off completely as the blood of Jesus is applied by faith. You are clean and whole again. Divine joy is restored and heaviness is taken away. Every atom of your being comes alive again and you are pulsating with the life of God.

There is nothing that deals effectively with sin in a man's life like the blood of Jesus. It is God's detergent for man's stained soul. It works effectively. It goes beyond the surface. It reaches deep down to the conscience and purges it from dead works to serve the true and living God. While explaining to the Hebrew believers the fact that the blood of Jesus Christ is God's only provision for man's sin-sick soul and that the blood of bulls and goats is nothing in comparison, Paul said:

> How much more shall the blood of Christ, who through the eternal Spirit offered himself without spot to God, purge your conscience from dead works to serve the living God?

Hebrews 9:14

Liberated Forever

Finally, the blood of Jesus, when applied, liberates you from the power of sin. Sin is a tyrant. It holds captive any soul that comes under its grip. This is why people continue in a sinful, terrible, destructive habit even when they are convinced it is wrong and are most willing to give it up. Until the blood of Jesus is faithfully applied, all your struggles to be free from sin through ordinary self-efforts will fail woefully. It may appear for some time that you are free. Then it happens again and you are back to square one. But with the blood of Jesus faithfully applied, the chain is broken and there is liberty. This is why the Bible says that for those who are under the New Testament made real by the blood of Christ, sin shall no longer dominate their lives. The dominion of sin over my life is broken for ever. I am no more its slave. I have been purchased by a new Master – Jesus Christ the Son of God. He paid with His life blood to set me free. I am free indeed and liberated forever.

> *For sin shall not have dominion over you: for ye are not under the law, but under grace.*
>
> Romans 6:14

Therefore beloved, the fountain of life is open to you. You can be cleansed of every stain. You can be completely whole. You can walk in holiness all the days of your life. Come to this fountain today and always. Let no stain remain upon your soul. That fountain was opened when Jesus' side was pierced at Calvary. It is still flowing fresh today. Hear what God says in His Word. Respond today and be free forever.

> *Come now, and let us reason together, saith the LORD: though your sins be as scarlet, they shall be as white as snow; though they be red like crimson, they shall be as wool.*
>
> Isaiah 1:18

Let me conclude with a quote from one of the saints of old, James Hamilton. This is what he said about the blood of Jesus.

> You that have faith in the fountain, frequent it.

Beware of two errors which are very natural and very disastrous. Beware of thinking that any sin is too small. There is no sin so little, but it may be germ of everlasting perdition. There is not a sin so enormous, but a drop of atoning blood will wash it away as utterly as if it were drowned in the depth of the sea.*

Make sure you do not close this chapter without turning to this fountain of life today.

* Quoted in *The Best of Dwight L. Moody* (Grand Rapids, MI: Baker Book House).

14

No Compromise!

After discovering that Jesus shed His precious blood to provide complete redemption for me, and that every aspect of my entire life for time and eternity was covered in this redemption, I made up my mind to settle for nothing less. I want to enjoy in full all that Jesus secured for me on the cross, and I will give no room to any bargaining with the adversary.

When Moses was to lead the people of Israel out of Egypt, Pharaoh, the king of Egypt was adamant. He did not want the people to go.

At first he wanted to use brutal force. He was not ready for negotiating. But through mighty signs and wonders God broke him down. Yet he was only ready to partially release Israel. He proffered all kinds of negotiation, just to keep Israel in bondage.

'OK, you can go, but do not go too far.'

'All right, please go, but leave your wives and children.'

'Take your wives and children, but leave your cattle behind.'

But Moses was not going to agree, neither was he going to compromise. 'Jehovah has ordered us to go, we will go with our wives, children, cattle and possessions; not a hoof shall be left behind,' Moses was insisting. He was resolute he wanted nothing but complete freedom for Israel.

While studying that scripture one day, the words of Moses struck me hard. *'Not an hoof shall be left behind.'* What a hard bargainer. He was not going to compromise Israel's total freedom. No, not for anything.

> *And Pharaoh called unto Moses, and said, Go ye, serve the LORD; only let your flocks and your herds be stayed: let your little ones also go with you. And Moses said, Thou must give us also sacrifices and burnt offerings, that we may sacrifice unto the LORD our God. Our cattle also shall go with us; there shall **not an hoof be left behind;** for thereof must we take to serve the LORD our God; and we know not with what we must serve the LORD, until we come thither.*
>
> Exodus 10:24–26 (my emphasis)

This is so true to life. The devil will want to negotiate our complete freedom.

'Well, you can be saved, but be sinning once in a while. After all God will forgive you.' He simply wants to rob you of your dominion over sin and the joy of the Lord as expressed in Romans 6:14.

> *For sin shall not have dominion over you: for ye are not under the law, but under grace.*

'Well, you are born again already, why make such a fuss over divine healing? After all the doctors have developed drugs that can take care of you. And if you die you are going to heaven, anyway.' Well, if Jesus paid for my healing then let me have it. I am not going to throw away what He paid for. I value and treasure it so much. It cost Him His life blood.

'Well, then, do not bother yourself about the material things of life. After all heaven is made of gold and if you are not careful, money will make you fall because money is the root of all evil.'

No way. The earth is the Lord's and the fullness thereof. If it belongs to my Father I am not going to leave it to Satan. Money is not the root of all evil, it is the love of money. My Father God can trust me to handle plenty of money for His kingdom without me loving it. Money shall not make me fall; I shall use it to spread abroad the knowledge of my God.

'What about this dominion stuff? Is that not New Age doctrine? You cannot have dominion while in the flesh. Wait until your resurrection or when you get to heaven and you can have as much dominion as you care for.'

Hold your lie Satan, no cheap bargain. My feet are on your neck already. I shall rule and reign over you in this life according to the word of my God. I am not waiting until I get to heaven for there is nothing to dominate there. It is here on earth that I will make the enemies of Jesus Christ to bow down.

> *Hold your lie Satan, no cheap bargain. My feet are on your neck already. I shall rule and reign over you in this life according to the word of my God.*

I am going to heaven to worship and serve my God for ever. This is not New Age, it is New Testament, sealed with the blood of Jesus, my Lord.

I have tried to put it in this graphic form to let you know that Satan will try to contest what Jesus purchased for you with His blood. Make up your mind.

There must be no compromise. Not a hoof shall be left behind. The Word of God must come to accurate fulfilment in your life. And it shall be unto you according to your faith.

15

He Spoke and I Was Free

He sent his word, and healed them,
And delivered them from their destructions.
Psalm 107:20

There were seven statements that Jesus Christ uttered while He was hanging upon the cross, His blood dripping to the ground removing every curse. These seven statements are critical and central to us understanding our redemption.

Personally, I believe there is a correlation between the seven sayings on the cross and the breaking of the seven seals of the book of Revelation.

Please understand that spiritual battles are battles of words. Spiritual authority is exercised by speaking. God spoke and the heavens and the earth were created. Jesus spoke and Lazarus came out of the grave. As our Lord Jesus spoke on the cross of Calvary, He was breaking the seals on that book, thereby unfolding God's redemption for us all.

He spoke and cancelled our debt of sin. He spoke and made a way for us to the throne of grace. He spoke and brought us into fellowship with Almighty God. He spoke and restored a paradise gloriously superior to the one the first Adam lost. He spoke and broke our chains. He spoke and I was free.

Out of those seven statements, three were

addressed to God, three were addressed to man, and
the last was a triumphant announcement to the whole
universe that He had perfectly accomplished the
Father's will.

Forgiveness Secured

Jesus' first statement on the cross was uttered to the
Father, an intercession that our debt of sins be forgiv-
en and cancelled.

> *Then said Jesus, Father, forgive them; for they know
> not what they do.*

Luke 23:34

When Jesus uttered these words He was not just
interceding for those crucifying Him, He was actually asking God the Father to extend His mercy and
grace upon all mankind. He was asking for man's sin
to be cancelled, that man might approach God freely and
receive the gift of eternal life.

*Understand that
spiritual battles
are battles of
words. Spiritual
authority is
exercised by
speaking. God
spoke and the
heavens and the
earth were created.*

'For they know not what they
do.' This statement expresses
accurately man's ignorance of
the full implications of sin.
Those crucifying Jesus knew
they were crucifying Him, but
they did not realise the gravity
or the implications of what they
were doing. No man yet fully
understands how seriously God
views sin. If we did, we would
not treat lightly any sin at all.
The Lord recently gave me an
insight into this that actually frightened me. Sin is

awful. It has terrible consequences. It leads to death and eternal separation from God.

God is holy. He cannot look on sin with any measure of approval. His holiness forbids Him to condone or excuse it or look the other way. Sin grieves the heart of God beyond measure and it must be visited with His fearful wrath. When God's sinless Son went to the cross, carrying our sins, He interceded for us to be forgiven by the Father, that we do not really understand how grievous our sins are in the sight of a Holy God. With that intercession mercy was released in the place of wrath and, at enormous cost, grace was made available to every man. The perfect, sinless Son of God bore your sins on His own body on the tree and called for God's pardon for your innumerable iniquities. Amazing grace!

> *For he hath made him to be sin for us, who knew no sin; that we might be made the righteousness of God in him.*
>
> II Corinthians 5:21

This becomes a glorious reality the moment you put your trust in the sacrifice of Jesus on the cross of Calvary. The moment you accept His blood as the ransom for your sins you receive God's pardon and cleansing freely.

The Power of Relationship

> *When Jesus therefore saw his mother, and the disciple standing by, whom he loved, he saith unto his mother, Woman behold thy son! Then saith he to the disciple, Behold thy mother! And from that hour that disciple took her unto his own home.*
>
> John 19:26–27

While Jesus was hanging on the cross he spoke to John the beloved the words above, committing His mother, Mary, to John's care. One would think at such a critical moment He might forget His mother. Not Jesus. He honoured her and committed her to the care of His closest disciple. This is instructive to all of us. We are to honour our *father and . . . mother; that thy days may be long upon the land . . .'* (Exodus 20:12). We are to provide for our household otherwise we are worse than infidels and have denied the faith. A casual reader of the Scriptures would think that Jesus did not pay much attention to His earthly parents. Aged twelve He was in the temple while they were searching all over the place for Him. He left them in order to preach and announced that only those who do the will of the Father are His brothers and mothers and sisters (Matthew 12:50). He said those who would follow Him must hate their fathers and mothers and take up their cross (Luke 14:26). Was He teaching us to abandon our parents and not care for them at all? No. As a matter of fact, He rebuked the Pharisees who would rather give to God what was meant for their parents, thereby using their tradition to make God's Word of no effect (Matthew 15:1–9). What Jesus taught us was to be so absolutely devoted to God that other commitments will be as nothing in comparison. However, we are to look after our parents and our household, to provide for them, even in times of emergencies.

The Water of Life Is Free

After this, Jesus knowing that all things were now accomplished, that the scripture might be fulfilled, saith, I thirst.

John 19:28

'I thirst.' Jesus said that on the cross, knowing that all things had been fulfilled. Then they soaked a sponge with vinegar and gave it to Him to drink.

He was thirsty so that you may drink of the water of life freely. On the cross He was completely exhausted and totally dehydrated. Yet there was no water to cool His tongue, rather He was given bitter vinegar.

One of the greatest pangs people suffer in hell is that of thirst. The rich man whose story our Lord Jesus told in Luke 16:24, longed for just a drop of water from the tip of Lazarus' finger to cool his tongue, but no one gave it to him. That was the experience of Jesus on the cross before He cried out, *'I thirst.'* Now the water of life is flowing. Those who have looked to the Lamb of Calvary in faith shall be refreshed for ever. He spoke and the water of life was made available for me.

> *Ho, every one that thirsteth, come ye to the waters, and he that hath no money; come ye, buy, and eat; yea, come, buy wine and milk without money and without price. Wherefore do ye spend money for that which is not bread? and your labour for that which satisfieth not? hearken diligently unto me, and eat ye that which is good, and let your soul delight itself in fatness.*
>
> Isaiah 55:1–2

You need to come to this water of life and buy, even though you have no money. How can you buy it without money? It was not money that made it available. It was love that cost Jesus His life. Hence, money cannot buy it. You must give Him your whole life in exchange.

> *And the Spirit and the bride say, Come. And let him*

*that heareth say, Come. And let him that is athirst
come. And whosoever will, let him take the water of
life freely.*

Revelation 22:17

Fellowship with the Father Restored

*And about the ninth hour Jesus cried with a loud
voice, saying, Eli, Eli, lama sabach-thani? that is to
say, My God, my God, why hast thou forsaken me?*

Matthew 27:46

In Eden, God drove man out of His presence at the fall. The beautiful fellowship the Father had with man was destroyed through sin. Because of God's holiness, He could do nothing else but separate and distance Himself from fallen man. His holiness required nothing less.

*Those who have
looked to the Lamb
of Calvary in faith
shall be refreshed
for ever. He spoke
and the water of
life was made
available for me.*

Prior to Jesus going to the cross, He had never broken fellowship with the Father. Never. He had never experienced sin, either by nature or practice. He was absolutely pure. In the Garden of Gethsemane when Jesus was praying, He knew that Calvary was drawing near. Our Lord knew that all our sins would be laid on Him and He would become a sin offering. He also knew that as soon as our sins came on Him the Father would take His eyes away from Him and they would be separated at that time. The very thought of coming into contact with our sins, and being separated from the Father filled

Him with horror and cost Him the keenest agony. To His pure nature and life, sin and a broken fellowship with the Father constitute such terrible, awful pain. He cried for the Father's help and consequently submitted to the Father's will.

On the cross it happened! With our sins laid on Him the Father turned away from the Son. The agony was unbearable. He cried out *'My God, my God, why hast thou forsaken me?'* As He became an offering for our sins, He made righteousness available to us. As He was separated from the Father, He made it possible for us to be united in fellowship with God. He made peace between us and the Father through the blood of His cross.

> But now in Christ Jesus ye who sometimes were far off are made nigh by the blood of Christ. For he is our peace, who hath made both one, and hath broken down the middle wall of partition between us; having abolished in his flesh the enmity, even the law of commandments contained in ordinances; for to make in himself of twain one new man, so making peace; and that he might reconcile both unto God in one body by the cross, having slain the enmity thereby.
>
> Ephesians 2:13–16

Paradise Restored

> And Jesus said unto him, Verily I say unto thee, To day shalt thou be with me in paradise.
>
> Luke 23:43

One of the two robbers crucified with our Lord Jesus was the first man to taste the fruit of redemption. The two men were convicts, guilty of felony. They deserved the just sentence passed on them according to the law of the land. They actually represent the two categories into which the whole of the human race is divided. *'For all have sinned, and have come short of the glory of God'* (Romans 3:23). Both had a first-hand opportunity to receive God's grace freely, even though they did not deserve it. One promptly seized the opportunity. Right there on the cross he begged for mercy. *'Lord, remember me when thou comest into thy kingdom'* (Luke 23:42). The answer was very prompt. *'Verily I say unto thee, To day shalt thou be with me in paradise'* (Luke 23:43).

> *As He became an offering for our sins, He made righteousness available to us. As He was separated from the Father, He made it possible for us to be united in fellowship with God. He made peace between us and the Father through the blood of His cross.*

The gates of heaven were flung wide open. This fellow was the first to enter in. The gates are still open to as many as refuse to trust in their own righteousness but instead cry to God for mercy. The self-righteous will not enter in. The religious will not go in. But as many as ask for God's mercy in sincere repentance will make it. As Jesus spoke those words, the doors of paradise opened, and they have remained open ever since. Whoever will, may come.

It is amazing that the second man rather than also crying for mercy, mocked his way into hell fire. This is the second category of the human race.

There are those who, in spite of all opportunities, shall still be lost forever in the lake of fire. I hope you are not one of them.

Safe for all Eternity

And when Jesus had cried with a loud voice, he said, Father, into thy hands I commend my spirit: and having said thus, he gave up the ghost.

Luke 23:46

'The eternal God is thy refuge,' declared Moses in Deuteronomy 33:27. Whether in living or in dying we are the Lord's. As Jesus was about to die on the cross, He committed the keeping of His spirit to God, our faithful Father who is able to keep till the very end. The devil did not drag Jesus' spirit to hell like some will want us to believe. Jesus committed His spirit to the Father. If He descended into hell, He must have gone there victorious, the Victor of Calvary, to lead captivity captive and to give gifts to men. God Almighty is our hiding place, our eternal refuge, our everlasting hope. As Jesus died on the cross, not only did He secure a place for us in the Father's heart, he made it possible for God to become our eternal refuge. If you commit yourself to God in faith and sincerity, you are safe and secure for all eternity and you will have nothing to fear all the days of your life.

It Is Finished

When Jesus therefore had received the vinegar, he said, It is finished: and he bowed his head, and gave up the ghost.

John 19:30

That was the triumphant declaration of our Lord

Jesus Christ as He hung on the cross. He had completed His assignment. He had finished the work of redemption. He had offered the perfect sacrifice and it was perfectly acceptable to the Father. The dominion of sin is ended. The rule of the enemy is ended. The oppression of the evil one is ended. It is finished. There is nothing more to add. By that one sacrifice Jesus perfected for ever those that are sanctified. It is finished.

> *He had completed His assignment. He had finished the work of redemption . . . The oppression of the evil one is ended. It is finished. There is nothing more to add. By that one sacrifice Jesus perfected for ever those that are sanctified. It is finished.*

This is heaven's verdict. You can receive an abundance of grace and enjoy the full benefit of redemption. Jesus our Lord secured it for us at enormous cost. He gave His life. He shed His blood. By faith you can key into Calvary and be free for ever. The dominion of sin is finished. The power of death is finished. The power of hell is finished. The Lamb of God shed His blood for me. The whole account of my sins, my guilt, my shame is settled for ever. It is finished. What a joyful, triumphant shout. What blessings are mine. The book of life is open. Complete redemption is fully available for me. It is finished.

16

His Blood Was Shed for Me

Likewise also the cup after supper, saying,
This cup is the new testament in my blood,
*which is **shed for you**.*
Luke 22:20 (my emphasis)

Matthew the Evangelist, in recording the accounts of the Passover night when Jesus spoke about His precious blood, put it this way:

*For this is my blood of the new testament, which is **shed for many** for the remission of sins.*
Matthew 26:28 (my emphasis)

Here our Lord Jesus Christ declared that His blood was **shed for many**.

Now, how many are these 'many' for whom the blood of Jesus was shed? We need to find out the answer in the Bible, God's Word, and not just from some incredible human opinions.

I was in Aba, Nigeria, recently for a Power Crusade. During the meeting, our Public Relations man arranged a meeting between me and a top media executive in the city. He was an adherent of the Grail Message, a metaphysical movement founded by one, Abdrushin. I shared the gospel with this man and particularly mentioned that the blood of Jesus was shed for him to remit his sin. He picked me up on that. Misquoting the above message in Matthew, he said the blood of Jesus was shed for many but not all; that there are some people for whom it was shed and there are a lot of others that were not covered in the plan. I took my time to straighten him out as we reasoned together, explaining to him from the Bible, the only authentic revelation of God to mankind.

For how many was the blood of Jesus shed? The answer is clear and simple from God's Word.

> *For God so loved the world, that he gave his only begotten Son, that **whosoever believeth in him** should not perish, but have everlasting life.*
> John 3:16 (my emphasis)

You can see that it is **the whole of mankind** that God so loved that He gave Jesus His only Son to die for. You can see also that **'whosoever'** or anyone of the human race who puts his or her trust in the atoning sacrifice of Jesus Christ upon the cross will not perish but have everlasting life.

> *For the scripture saith, **Whosoever believeth on him** shall not be ashamed. For there is no difference between the Jew and the Greek: for the same Lord over all is rich unto all that call upon him.*
> Romans 10:11–12 (my emphasis)

This is another scripture that proves that Jesus shed His precious blood for all the world. He shed it for Jews and Gentiles alike. He shed His blood for the white, the red and the black. He shed His blood for Africans, Hispanics, Asians, Arabs, Europeans, Americans, Japanese and every single person of the human race. As far as redemption is concerned, there is no difference between the Jews and the Gentiles or among any of the Gentile race. The same blood is shed for all. The same God is rich towards all that call upon Him.

> *For whosoever shall call upon the name of the Lord shall be saved.* Romans 10:13

Let us take a look at another scripture.

> *The next day John seeth Jesus coming unto him, and saith, Behold the Lamb of God, which taketh away* **the sin of the world.**
> John 1:29 (my emphasis)

Here again it is made plain. Jesus Christ is the Lamb of God slain for the sin of the entire world. He is the only One that can take away our sin. The blood He shed covers every single person that has ever walked on earth, from Adam to the last person that will ever live on earth. While the door of God's mercy still remains open, you can always take advantage of the precious blood of Jesus, the Lamb of God.

Let us examine another scripture now:

> *For this is good and acceptable in the sight of God our Saviour;* **who will have all men to be saved,** *and to come unto the knowledge of the truth.*
> *For there is one God, and one mediator between God and men, the man Christ Jesus.*
> I Timothy 2:3–5 (my emphasis)

Many vital points emerge from this passage. First, there is only one true and living God who is the Creator of all mankind and everything there is. He is the Father of our Lord Jesus Christ. This God does not want any man to perish and go to hell. He wants all men to be saved.

There is only one Mediator between God and man and this is the man Jesus Christ. Jesus Christ has reconciled all men to God by giving His life. How did He give His life? By shedding His blood, because the life of the flesh is in the blood. If there is only one God, and He wants all men to be saved; if there is only one Mediator between God and man and He shed His blood that all men may be saved, then the blood of Jesus has been shed for all men to be saved.

The Lord Jesus Himself made it plain that He is the only Redeemer of mankind. When the people were seeking Him for more bread and fishes, having tasted the ones He produced miraculously, He told them:

> *Labour not for the meat which perisheth, but for that meat which endureth unto everlasting life, which the Son of man shall give unto you: for him hath God the Father sealed.*

John 6:27

Please take note: *'for him hath God the Father sealed'.* He is the only One upon whom the Father put the seal of divine approval. He is the only Saviour of the world, and He made this plain in several places.

> *Jesus saith unto him, I am the way, the truth, and the life: no man cometh unto the Father, but by me.*

John 14:6

May I put this on record: there has never been a man in existence who claimed to be the only way to God and whose message actually had that ring of truth. Only Jesus.

No wonder Peter proclaimed so boldly that there is no other way to get to God except by Jesus and His precious blood:

Neither is there salvation in any other: for there is none other name under heaven given among men, whereby we must be saved.

Acts 4:12

Peter was speaking out of deep conviction borne out of actual personal experience.

When Jesus began to speak about the necessity of man eating His flesh and drinking His blood, most of His followers went back. They did not understand this 'blood' issue and were offended. Jesus turned to those remaining including Peter, and asked, *'Will ye also go away?'*

Then Simon Peter answered him, Lord, to whom shall we go? thou hast the words of eternal life. And we believe and are sure that thou art that Christ, the Son of the living God.

John 6:68–69

'To whom shall we go? You have the words of eternal life! We believe and are sure that You are that Christ, the Son of the living God.' Blessed words indeed.

What more? The blood of Jesus Christ, God's Son, was shed for all the world. None is excluded. God's salvation plan covers every single person on the face of the earth.

Personally Applied

Having established the fact that the blood of Jesus was shed for all the world, it is important to

> *There has never been a man in existence who claimed to be the only way to God and whose message actually had that ring of truth. Only Jesus.*

make it clear that it becomes effective only when it is personally applied. This is the truth that is being so powerfully revealed in both the accounts of Matthew and Luke, when the scriptures are compared.

> *For this is my blood of the new testament, which is **shed for many** for the remission of sins.*
> Matthew 26:28 (my emphasis)

> *Likewise also the cup after supper, saying, This cup is the new testament in my blood, which is **shed for you**.*
> Luke 22:20 (my emphasis)

While Matthew says the blood that was shed covers everyone on earth, Luke says it works only when it is personally applied. The blood of Jesus will do you no good until you know, believe and confess that it was specifically shed for you. **The blood of Jesus was shed for me.** This is a powerful confession of faith.

You will experience the power that is in the blood of Jesus only after you have personally applied it by faith.

You know that even when there is plenty of water, soap, body cream and deodorants, some people still go about dirty and smelly, not for lack of soap, water or deodorant. My friend, if you are not going to smell, you have to personally use these items on your body correctly. If you do not, you will smell bad.

In the same way, people can be bound to sin, tormented by Satan, afflicted in the world and then end up in the lake of fire, not because the blood of Jesus is not available to them; not because they are not included in God's great plan of salvation, but simply because they have not personally applied the blood of Jesus on their spirit and soul. The blood of Jesus is God's only remedy for man's sin and fall. You will experience the power that is in the blood of Jesus only after you have personally applied it by faith.

Therefore beloved, believe it firmly in your heart, and confess it loudly with your mouth: **The blood of Jesus was shed for me.**

A Most Vivid Confession

What you say with your mouth is vital, because the power of life and death is in the tongue (Proverbs 18:21). Jesus Christ our Lord said that by your words you shall be justified and by your words you shall be condemned (Matthew 12:37). Essentially, spiritual battles are battles of words. You either speak the right, positive words of faith and win or you speak the wrong, negative words of fear and you lose. Speaking the right words at the right time is a vital element of living the victorious life. '*How forcible are right words!*' (Job 6:25).

What you say with your mouth is vital, because the power of life and death is in the tongue ... You either speak the right, positive words of faith and win or you speak the wrong, negative words of fear and you lose. Speaking the right words at the right time is a vital element of living the victorious life.

When David met Goliath in combat, he won with words. The battle was not decided by David's sling and five stones. He had

actually killed Goliath with prophetic words of faith
before the stone finished off the job! Learn to overcome the adversary by speaking strong, positive
words. The Bible says we overcome not only by the
blood of the Lamb but also by the word of our testimony or the words of our confession:

> *And they overcame him by the blood of the Lamb,*
> *and by the word of their testimony; and they loved*
> *not their lives unto the death.*
>
> Revelation 12:11

What does this mean? The blood of Jesus has to
become a strong confession of faith held out against
the adversary to push him out of your life. **The blood
of Jesus was shed for me.**

Whenever the devil wants to remind you of your
past, you remind him of the blood. When you say
'The blood of Jesus was shed for me', you are saying
to Satan: 'Keep your filthy mouth shut, my past is
already covered by the blood of Jesus and you have
no business with it!'

When the enemy wants to bring an affliction or a
sickness upon your body and you declare, **'The
blood of Jesus was shed for me',** you are saying to
Satan: 'This body does not belong to you anymore! It
has been bought by Jesus Christ. Therefore, you cannot make me sick, because the blood of Jesus was
shed for me.'

You can apply this to any area of your life. The
blood of Jesus settles all argument with Satan. He
may argue with your theology or your doctrinal
belief. He may even argue with your experiences and
try to make you doubt. But he has no answer to the
blood of Jesus! Absolutely none. Therefore, use the

blood against him. Stand on redemption ground and rejoice in what Jesus has done for you. You cannot fail when you do. Remember: **the blood of Jesus was shed for you.**

17

The Blood that Speaks I

*But ye are come unto . . . Jesus the mediator of the
new covenant, and to the blood of sprinkling, that
speaketh better things than that of Abel.*
Hebrews 12:22,24

The blood of Jesus Christ is living and it speaks.
The Bible says that all who believe in Christ and
are born again have come to this blood, and it speaks
for us before God.

When Cain killed his brother Abel, he buried him,
thinking nobody would find out.

But though Abel was dead, his blood was speaking out. God said to Cain, '. . . *the voice of thy brother's
blood crieth unto me from the ground'* (Genesis 4:10b).
The blood of Abel was speaking against Cain.
Everywhere Cain went he kept hearing the blood saying, 'Vengeance! Judgment! Death!' Cain was set
apart for his sins and he paid the penalty with his
own blood; even now he is still in hell-fire.

But the blood of Jesus Christ speaks better things
than the blood of Abel. Just as Abel's blood spoke
after he was killed, the blood of Jesus Christ is still
speaking two thousand years after it was shed for us.
Whereas the blood of Abel cried for vengeance, we
can hear the blood of Jesus pleading on our behalf
'Mercy! Pardon! Grace! Life!' Glory be to God for the

blood of Jesus Christ. We have mercy, pardon, grace, acceptance and life through that blood. The blood is still speaking on your behalf.

What Happens when a Believer Sins?

This is a vital question we have to face. What does the Bible teach on this? What is the Holy Spirit saying to us? What should our attitude be, both to another believer who has been overtaken by a fault as well as if it happens to us personally?

First, it must be clear that it is not the will of God that a believer should fall into sin. He has spoken clearly in His word: *'My little children, these things write I unto you, that ye sin not'* (I John 2:1). That ye sin not. This is God's will. This is why He gave us His Word.

> *Wherewithal shall a young man cleanse his way?*
> *By taking heed thereto according to thy word.*
>
> Psalm 119:9

> *Thy word have I hid in mine heart,*
> *That I might not sin against thee.*
>
> Psalm 119:11

> *Blessed are the undefiled in the way,*
> *Who walk in the law of the LORD.*
> *Blessed are they that keep his testimonies,*
> *And that seek him with the whole heart.*
> *They also do no iniquity:*
> *They walk in his ways.*
>
> Psalm 119:1–3

Even though the author of Psalm 119 wrote it in genuine repentance and penitence, he refused to compromise the fact that God's will for us is a life of holi-

ness and complete victory over sin. He refused to let
his experience of failure get in the way of God's
Word. He acknowledged that it is possible to be
'*undefiled in the way*', that it is possible for a young
man to '*keep his way pure*' (and if a young man can,
then an older man can. More so, for the youth, being
immature, are more prone to the '*sins of my youth*',
whereas the older ones, having slowed down in their
quest for adventure, and having seen the vanity of a
life of sin, are more sober, more reflective and more
self-controlled). He acknowledged that by keeping
God's Word in one's heart it is possible not to sin
against God.

We must never judge God's Word by our experience, rather we must judge our experience by God's
word and make it line up with His Word. Our experiences may be false. They are subjective. God's Word
is true. It is objective. '*Yea, let God be true, but every
man a liar*' (Romans 3:4a).

Even though this man had experienced the failure
of falling into sin, yet he made
it so clear that God's standard
is that we do not sin, and this is
quite possible if we set our
hearts on it as Daniel did; if we
receive grace for it like Paul
and if we keep the Word of
God in our heart at all times.

> *Whereas the blood
> of Abel cried for
> vengeance, we can
> hear the blood of
> Jesus pleading on
> our behalf 'Mercy!
> Pardon! Grace!
> Life!'*

'*That ye sin not.*' This is
God's will for us and He has
made abundant provision for
us in His Word to make this
possible. We can stand on the
Word of God and He will keep us spotless and deliv-

er us from every temptation.

> *There hath no temptation taken you but such as is common to man: but God is faithful, who will not suffer you to be tempted above that ye are able; but will with the temptation also make a way to escape, that ye may be able to bear it.*
>
> I Corinthians 10:13

Jesus Christ died to save us from our sins, and no genuine believer makes a habit of sinning.

Falling into sin should, to a believer, be like having an accident with your car. There are people who never have an accident at all until they change their car or wear it out. They do not want it to happen and when it does they feel very unhappy about it. And of course they do not have accidents every day of their lives. A man who gets involved in accidents again and again is dangerous to himself and to other road users. This is the picture of a man living in sin.

We must never judge God's Word by our experience, rather we must judge our experience by God's Word and make it line up with His Word. Our experiences may be false. They are subjective. God's Word is true. It is objective.

Sin is pleasurable to an unbeliever. But when you are born again Christ takes the pleasure out of sin. He becomes your joy and salvation and all in all. If there is anyone who claims to be born again and still lives habitually in sin, enjoying sinful pleasures and not living in holiness and commitment to Christ, not willing to break away from all that is sinful, dirty, unethical, immoral and questionable; his claim of being saved must be false. The Bible says:

> Whosoever abideth in him sinneth not: whosoever sinneth hath not seen him, neither known him.
>
> I John 3:6

Claiming to be born again and still living in sin do not go together. We are to be holy as He who has called us is holy.

Falling into sin should, to a believer, be like having an accident with your car ... A man who gets involved in accidents again and again is dangerous to himself and to other road users. This is the picture of a man living in sin.

> But as he which hath called you is holy, so be ye holy in all manner of conversation.
>
> I Peter 1:15

If a Man Does Sin

Having said all this, it must be acknowledged that we are still in the flesh; we live in a world that is hostile to the gospel and exerts pressure on us; and we face daily conflicts and temptations from the devil.

It is possible for a believer to fall into sin. When this happens, is that the end of the road? No. You have the blood of Jesus Christ pleading for you before the throne of mercy and you can be forgiven, cleansed and fully restored into fellowship with God again.

Sin breaks your fellowship with God. It tends to quench the Spirit. It gives Satan opportunities to harass and attack you. It will bring guilt, condemnation and depression, but you should never forget God's provision. Take advantage of the blood of Jesus Christ immediately.

> *My little children, these things write I unto you, that ye sin not. And if any man sin, we have an advocate with the Father, Jesus Christ the righteous: and he is the propitiation for our sins: and not for ours only, but also for the sins of the whole world.*
>
> I John 2:1–2

Please note God's Word: *If* any man sin, not *when* any man sin. It is a matter of *if*, not *when*. Believers falling into sin is a possibility, but should not be the norm. Living like Christ should be the norm after we are born again. However, God has made adequate provision for a believer who does fall into sin to be forgiven, cleansed and fully restored.

If you happen to fall into sin, you should genuinely repent of the sin immediately and confess it to God. Remember, repentance involves confession of the sins and a determination to forsake them.

> *He that covereth his sins shall not prosper:*
> *But whoso confesseth and forsaketh them shall have mercy.*
>
> Proverbs 28:13

You should by faith plead the blood of Jesus upon yourself. This is the only way you can be rid of sin and have God's forgiveness. Nothing but the blood of Jesus. It is not your tears that will cleanse you. Yes, shed the tears of sorrow for sin and let godly sorrow lead you to true repentance. But your faith must be in the cleansing blood, not in your tears.

It is not your works, or fasting, or self-affliction

that will cleanse you. Sometimes an overriding sense of guilt drives us to afflict ourselves mercilessly for the sin committed, thereby hoping for a relief. Afflicting yourself will do nothing if you do not have faith in the blood. Remember, the blood has been shed for you. This blood will speak for you before God, cleanse you from every defilement and purify your conscience from all guilt.

> *How much more shall the blood of Christ, who through the eternal Spirit offered himself without spot to God, purge your conscience from dead works to serve the living God?*
>
> Hebrews 9:14

Do not make the mistake of thinking that a sin is too small for the blood. No sin is too small: it is the seed of eternal perdition. Neither should you think a sin is so great or grievous that the blood of Jesus cannot fully cleanse it and blot it out. God says *'Come now, and let us reason together . . . though your sins be as scarlet, they shall be as white as snow; though they be red like crimson, they shall be as wool'* (Isaiah 1:18). The blood of Jesus will blot out all sins that are brought to it in sincere confession and genuine repentance.

When God forgives, He forgets. He does not hold those sins and iniquities against you any more. They are not just buried under the blood of Jesus Christ, they have been purged and blotted out. They do not exist any more as far as God is concerned. This is how powerful the blood of Jesus is.

There are many people who still live in the memory of their bitter past. They sinned against God, repented and trusted the blood of Jesus for cleansing, but while God forgave them, they have not been able to forgive themselves. They still allow the devil to load them with guilt and bitterness.

When you sincerely repent of any sin, God forgives. If God has forgiven you please forgive yourself and let the Holy Spirit fill you with divine joy again. I shall share three scriptures with you on this:

> *I, even I, am he that blotteth out thy transgressions for mine own sake, and will not remember thy sins. Put me in remembrance: let us plead together: declare thou, that thou mayest be justified.*
>
> Isaiah 43:25–26

It is not your works, or fasting, or self-affliction that will cleanse you. Sometimes an overriding sense of guilt drives us to afflict ourselves mercilessly for the sin committed, thereby hoping for a relief. Afflicting yourself will do nothing if you do not have faith in the blood.

God says that when you confess your sins and sincerely ask for cleansing through the blood of Jesus, He blots out your sins. He blots them out, not for your own righteousness or goodness, but for His own sake; because of the blood of Jesus. Now that those sins are blotted out you can pray, plead your case and receive your miracles from God. You can always take God at His word.

> *If we say that we have no sin, we deceive ourselves, and the truth is not in us. If we confess our sins, he is faithful and just to forgive us our sins, and to cleanse us from all unrighteousness.*
>
> I John 1:8–9

Here the Bible says you should face your sins, own up to them and sincerely confess them to God. God says when you do that He will do two things; forgive your sins and cleanse you from all unrighteousness, because of His faithfulness and justice. He ties our forgiveness to His key attributes; faithfulness and justice. This, to me, is awesome. It is only when God ceases to be faithful and just that He will not forgive and cleanse the sin that has been repented of and brought for cleansing with the blood of Jesus. Simply put, this makes me tremble at the goodness of God and I realize how true the words of David are:

> *When God forgives, He forgets. He does not hold those sins and iniquities against you any more. They are not just buried under the blood of Jesus Christ they have been purged and blotted out. They do not exist any more as far as God is concerned.*

Out of the depths have I cried
* unto thee, O LORD.*
Lord, hear my voice:
Let thine ears be attentive
To the voice of my supplications.
If thou, LORD, shouldest mark
* iniquities,*
O Lord, who shall stand?
But there is forgiveness with
* thee,*
That thou mayest be feared.
Psalm 130:1–4

Thanks be to God! Because He is faithful and just; because of the precious blood of Jesus there is total forgiveness and deep cleansing for you.

For this is the covenant that I will make with the
* house of Israel*
After those days, saith the Lord;

I will put my laws into their mind,
And write them in their hearts:
And I will be to them a God,
And they shall be to me a people . . .
For I will be merciful to their unrighteousness,
And their sins and their iniquities will I
remember no more.

Hebrews 8:10,12 (my emphasis)

The blood of Jesus is the blood of the new covenant (Hebrews 13:20). One of the terms of the new covenant is that the cleansing is so thorough and the forgiveness so real that God will never again remember those sins you have repented of, because of the blood of Jesus.

Therefore, beloved, if you have repented of those sins indeed, God has forgiven you. There is nothing against you any more. The whole account is settled. You are free; through the blood of Jesus! Go and sin no more, for sin shall no longer have dominion over you, because the blood of Jesus was shed for you.

18

The Blood that Speaks II

Brethren, if any of you do err from the truth,
and one convert him; let him know, that he which
converteth the sinner from the error of his way
shall save a soul from death, and shall hide
a multitude of sins.
James 5:19–20

What happens if a believer falls into sin? We have looked at what the attitude of the individual should be to himself and the sin. Now what should be the attitude of the brethren, the church and spiritual leadership? The Bible is very clear on this. As soon as it is known, we should call the person involved, confront him or her with the sin in meekness and love, yet jealous for God's holiness. Our goal should not be to punish, expose or humiliate him or her, but to restore the person back to the Lord and to the brethren. In dealing with sin we must be firm and principled, but not critical, judgmental or unkind. We must be angry at sin and the enemy behind it, but we must see the fellow believer as a prey that needs to be delivered out of the hands of the adversary.

If the person involved has truly repented of the sin, if he has made his way right with God and there is evidence of genuine repentance, we should freely forgive and love that person warmly again without holding anything against him. If we expect to receive mercy from God we must extend mercy to others.

If the person has not repented, but is convicted and sincerely acknowledges the evil of his deed, then we should rebuke him in love and lead him to repentance. If you are not qualified to handle the case, then refer it to people who have the spiritual oversight of the person. But in all of this you must walk in the fear of the Lord, lest you yourself play into the hands of the devil. This is what the Bible says:

> *Brethren, if a man be overtaken in a fault, ye which are spiritual, restore such an one in the spirit of meekness; considering thyself, lest thou also be tempted.*

> Galatians 6:1

The Lord taught me a lesson on this in a practical way in 1976. There was a minister of the gospel in our area, a popular evangelist, who fell into sin. After the incident, whenever I heard him or heard his name mentioned I had a cold, critical, judgmental attitude.

One Sunday after the service, I was talking with a brother when this evangelist's name came up in our conversation. The old feelings rose up in me again and I could not really continue the discussion. I was upset and angry.

'How could he have done that?' I thought. 'We all looked up to him. I will not have anything to do with him again. I want to keep myself pure,' I concluded within myself. That was July 1976.

After I left the brother I was talking with, the Spirit of the Lord spoke so clearly to me I could not mistake it.

'He is my servant, and he indeed sinned against

me,' the Lord said very, very clearly.

'He has since made his way right and I have forgiven him. Who are you to have a judgmental attitude against my servant?'

The voice of the Lord was so clear. It was now my
turn to repent. I have since loved to see, hear and
appreciate that tremendous man of God. I chose not
to judge him by his past failure. I decided to extend
mercy to him so that I might find mercy before the
Lord. After all, he did not continue in sin. He had
repented and God had accepted him. I cannot imagine myself in his situation, but I want to work out my
salvation with fear and trembling knowing that we
all depend on the mercy of God.

Restore Him Back Again

All those who God has forgiven should enjoy the
confidence of their brethren. We are in a battle against
our enemy. I have never seen an army that shoots its
wounded soldiers. Rather, they rally round, give the
wounded first aid – the best treatment that will help
them recover as soon as possible. So we are not to slay
our wounded soldiers; rather we should rally round
and help them to live again.

We are to restore such a one in the spirit of meekness and love, with due consideration that it could
have happened to any of us. That was exactly what
the apostle Paul wrote to the Galatian brethren:

> *Brethren, if a man be overtaken in a fault, ye which
> are spiritual, restore such an one in the spirit of
> meekness; considering thyself, lest thou also be
> tempted. Bear ye one another's burdens, and so ful-
> fil the law of Christ.*

Galatians 6:1,2

Our attitude to a Christian who falls into sin is not to broadcast it or 'pass the word around'. Our first duty is to seek to restore such a one as soon as possible, thereby delivering our brother or sister from the grip of Satan. If he shows evidence of true repentance and remorse we are to pray with him and restore him to fellowship without delay. He may have to take some discipline. If he is a minister, he may have to stay out of ministry work for some time depending on the gravity of the case. This should be handled by mature men of God or a respected spiritual leader. The pastor, or the minister who has direct spiritual oversight over him or her, should assume this responsibility as soon as the case is known. If his repentance is genuine and his restoration is complete then we have won our brother and the devil has lost again! Jesus is glorified that the straying sheep has come home. This is the ultimate goal of every spiritual discipline imposed. This should be the ultimate aim of the minister or spiritual leader handling the case. You must not break a bruised reed or quench a smoking flax (Isaiah 42:3). Be careful not to allow a negative, religious spirit ruin your fellow believer who is truly penitent. What you do today is a seed that you plant for your own tomorrow. *'Blessed are the merciful: for they shall obtain mercy'* (Matthew 5:7). This has been my attitude since July 1976, as taught by the Holy Spirit and I am sure it agrees with the spirit of the New Testament.

I have been taught by God to see life as a matter of sowing and reaping. Whatever I do to my brother is a seed I am sowing. Due season will soon come when I shall reap my harvest. I want to sow in righteousness and mercy so that I may reap a multiple of the same. Even when I find myself in a situation where discipline has to be imposed on a brother or sister or a fellow minister for his or her sinful acts, no matter how hard and tough the discipline, I still make sure I do it in love (there is tough love) with the singular purpose of restoring and not destroying the person involved. He is a precious child of God for whom Jesus Christ shed His precious blood. It is only after every avenue of restoration is explored and the man still remains impenitent that I give up; never before.

> We are in a battle against our enemy. I have never seen an army that shoots its wounded soldiers. Rather, they rally round, give the wounded first aid – the best treatment that will help them recover as soon as possible. So we are not to slay our wounded soldiers; rather, we should rally round and help them to live again.

The Unrepentant Sinner

Supposing the person refuses to acknowledge his fault and feels no need for repentance? Suppose he even boasts and gloats over his sin? Then we should allow spiritual leaders to handle the case and administer such scriptural discipline that is calculated to produce genuine repentance in him – never to destroy him. In the case of an impenitent person, the body of Christ must be protected from corruption and contamination. Remember *'a little leaven leaveneth the whole lump'* (I Corinthians 5:6b) and spiritual leaders must move into action. If the case is proved to be true and he refuses to repent, appropriate biblical sanctions should be imposed. This may even mean disfellowship or excommunication depending on the nature of the case. The Church is not to keep company with false brethren living in sin who refuse to truly repent.

There was once a case like this in the Corinthian church. The apostle Paul wrote about it under the inspiration of the Holy Spirit and gave a clear direction on what was to be done. This is the duty of every genuine spiritual leader. It is our duty to see that the body of Christ is kept pure and undefiled.

> *It is reported commonly that there is fornication among you, and such fornication as is not so much as named among the Gentiles, that one should have his father's wife. And ye are puffed up, and have not rather mourned, that he that hath done this deed might be taken away from among you. For I verily, as absent in body, but present in spirit, have judged already, as though I were present, concerning him that hath so done this deed, in the name of our Lord Jesus Christ, when ye are gathered together, and my spirit, with the power of our Lord Jesus Christ, to deliver such an one unto Satan for the destruction of the flesh, that the spirit may be saved in the day of the Lord Jesus.*

I Corinthians 5:1–5

The man in question was living in the terrible sin of adultery and was neither sober nor repentant.

Paul advised that the man should be disfellowshipped and handed over to Satan for the 'destruction of the flesh'. Why? *'That the spirit may be saved in the day of the Lord'*. Even though severe punishment was imposed, Paul had in view the ultimate salvation of this man.

Of course the tough discipline imposed broke the

man down and he became truly sorry for his sin.

As soon as the man was moved to repentance and it was obvious to all, Paul wrote again that he be received by all and shown much love again. The purpose of the initial discipline had been achieved.

> *I have been taught by God to see life as a matter of sowing and reaping. Whatever I do to my brother is a seed I am sowing. Due season will soon come when I shall reap my harvest. I want to sow in righteousness and mercy so that I may reap a multiple of the same.*

Sufficient to such a man is this punishment, which was inflicted of many. So that contrariwise ye ought rather to forgive him, and comfort him, lest perhaps such a one should be swallowed up with overmuch sorrow. Wherefore I beseech you that ye would confirm your love toward him.

II Corinthians 2:6–8

Supposing the person, having been confronted with the proven case of sin and iniquity, refuses to repent, rejects all attempts by spiritual leaders to restore him, and ignores spiritual discipline, what do we do? Such a person should not only be disfellowshipped, but regarded as an unbeliever. The apostle Paul said:

I wrote unto you in an epistle not to company with fornicators: yet not altogether with the fornicators of this world, or with the covetous, or extortioners, or with idolaters; for then must ye needs go out of the world. But now I have written unto you not to keep company, if any man that is called a brother be a for-

nicator, or covetous, or an idolater, or a railer, or a drunkard, or an extortioner; with such an one no not to eat. For what have I to do to judge them also that are without? do not ye judge them that are within? But them that are without God judgeth. Therefore put away from among yourselves that wicked person.

I Corinthians 5:9–13

There was the case of a pastor in Lagos. He discovered that a lady member of his church was living immorally with a man from another church, who was married and had a family of five. He spent much time counselling this young lady. She promised to change but did not. Then the pastor went to meet with the married man and talked to him together with the lady. They promised to stop the unholy affair, but did not. The pastor tried to involve the pastor of the man's church, but it is so large that he could not get the pastor's attention.

When it became clear the lady was not going to quit sinning and leave this man, the pastorate decided to disfellowship her from the church. Some leaders raised objections that the church might split as a result, because the lady was very prominent; but after

Supposing the person, having been confronted with the proven case of sin and iniquity, refuses to repent, rejects all attempts by spiritual leaders to restore him, and ignores spiritual discipline, what do we do? Such a person should not only be disfellowshipped, but regarded as an unbeliever.

much prayer the senior pastor went ahead.

She was called up one Sunday during the service and sent out of the church with a strong rebuke. The Holy Spirit took over. Rather than anger and resentment, fear fell on all the members of the church. Everyone sat up and straightened out their spiritual lives, and the church began to grow rapidly. The unbelievers around heard what had happened and developed great respect for the church.

What if there is a dispute or disagreement and hurt between two brothers or sisters? What do you do when you discover that your brother has sinned against you, or you have something against your brother in your heart?

Jesus Christ our Lord said if a brother sins against you, go and meet him all alone and resolve the issue. If he will not hear you, take two witnesses along and talk to him. If he still will not hear, take him to the elders of the church. If he will not listen to the church leaders, then regard him as an infidel, as an unbeliever. You are not to hate him, or be bitter against him (bitterness and hatred are sins on their own) but you need not have anything to do with him. Disfellowship him yet love and pray for him that God may grant him repentance:

> *Moreover if thy brother shall trespass against thee, go and tell him his fault between thee and him alone: if he shall hear thee, thou hast gained thy brother. But if he will not hear thee, then take with thee one or two more, that in the mouth of two or three witnesses every word may be established. And if he shall neglect to hear them, tell it unto the church: but if he neglect to hear the church, let him be unto thee as an heathen man and a publican. Verily I say*

unto you, Whatsoever ye shall bind on earth shall be bound in heaven: and whatsoever ye shall loose on earth shall be loosed in heaven.

Matthew 18:15–18

A man that is an heretick after the first and second admonition reject; knowing that he that is such is subverted, and sinneth, being condemned of himself.

Titus 3:10–11

There is a need to bring discipline back into the Church so that the fear of God may be in the hearts of people. We need to teach believers to detest sin and maintain a life of purity.

We must not take the precious blood of Jesus Christ for granted. Sin in the body of Christ must be handled in the light of the Word of God so that the Church may become strong and vibrant, doing the will of God on earth and representing Jesus Christ our Lord worthily. False brethren must be rejected out of the body and false ministers exposed for who they are. Where there is genuine repentance, we should apply faith in the blood of Jesus and, in love and humility, bring restoration to the fallen. There is power in the blood of Jesus to restore the fallen and to make them strong again. That was what gave Peter hope after he denied the Lord three times. But Judas Iscariot had no hope, because there was no genuine repentance in his heart.

There is power in the blood of Jesus to deliver, to cleanse and to restore.

19

The Blood of the New Testament

For this is my blood of the new testament,
which is shed for many for the remission of sins.
Matthew 26:28

It must be emphasized that the blood of Jesus is the blood of the New Testament. Many people today live as though we are still under the Old Testament. They relate to the blood of Jesus just as the Old Testament saints related to the blood of bulls, goats or heifers of the old covenant. They approach the Christian life from a ritualistic, legalistic point of view. The result is that they never find the joy, the thrill of walking in the grace of God and in the fellowship of the Holy Spirit.

We all need to realize that the law was the basis of relating to God only until the time of John the Baptist. Grace and truth came by the Lord Jesus.

The law and the prophets were until John: since that time the kingdom of God is preached, and every man presseth into it.

Luke 16:16

Jesus came to fulfil the law. He came to institute an era of grace through the truth of God's Word. He did this by His precious blood which He shed. The blood of the New Testament is the blood of grace. Grace is the hallmark of the New Testament. We are saved by grace alone. And we are kept by the power of God.

Therefore, beloved, you are in a new era – an era of grace and divine favour. Even though the law is not abrogated, it no longer saves anyone. It was our guide until the grace of God was revealed in Christ. Through faith in our Lord Jesus Christ, you can stand fast in the grace of God.

Leviticus or Acts

I will never forget reading through the book of Leviticus for the first time after I was born again. As I read through the seemingly endless list of rituals, sacrifices, rules and demands of the laws of the Old Testament, I became gratefully aware of what the blood of Jesus Christ has done for me – liberating me from the rigorous demands of those endless rituals; redeeming me to live by faith through grace; allowing me to enjoy the benefits of redemption in the comfort of the Holy Spirit! But today some people still live in the book of Leviticus. To them Christianity is all rituals, sacrifices, burnt offerings, altars and incense in the literal sense. They need to know that the blood of Jesus has settled all of that and has initiated a new and glorious way for us. They need to change their address from Leviticus to Acts of the Apostles. Not only that, they need to change their thinking and line up with New Testament reality. God no longer requires those rituals to justify anyone. We are justified freely by our faith in the Lord Jesus Christ.

The early apostles had to deal with this issue at one time. There were Jewish believers who insisted that new believers who were Gentiles should observe all the law of Moses before they could be considered saved. They failed to differentiate between the blood of Jesus and the blood of the Old Testament. As far as they were concerned, there was no difference.

Then the apostles took time to pray and seek the face of God. They said, *'Now therefore why tempt ye God, to put a yoke upon the neck of the disciples, which neither our fathers nor we were able to bear'* (Acts 15:10). They found that the blood of Jesus has released us from the yoke of legalism and bondage and has justified us *'from all things, from which ye could not be justified by the law of Moses'* (Acts 13:39).

It cannot be over-emphasized that the blood of Jesus has released us from the bondage of religious legalism. The righteous demands of the law can now be fulfilled in all who walk by faith, putting their trust in the blood of Jesus . . . the blood of the New Testament.

There are certain characteristics of the blood of the New Testament that we need to bring out clearly in contrast with the blood of the Old.

The blood of the New Testament is the blood of grace. Grace is the hallmark of the New Testament. We are saved by grace alone. And we are kept by the power of God.

Not the Blood of Animals

In the Old Testament, it was the blood of animals that was used for sacrifices and offerings for sin. However, the Bible makes it plain that the blood of these animals could not take away sins.

For it is not possible that the blood of bulls and of goats should take away sins.

Hebrews
10:4 (my emphasis)

Remember, the blood of these animals only **covered** or **atoned** for the sins of the people. It did not have the power to blot out sin and release grace for victory. God only allowed that situation until the blood of the New Testament was shed to take away sin once and for all.

Yet the Old Testament saints were blessed. David described their blessedness in the book of Psalms:

> *Blessed is he whose transgression is forgiven, whose sin is covered.*
> *Blessed is the man unto whom the LORD imputeth not iniquity,*
> *And in whose spirit there is no guile.*
>
> Psalm 32:1–2

They considered themselves happy, fortunate and to be envied because their sins were covered and they obtained mercy and forgiveness from God. Reading the Amplified Bible translation of that passage you will realize they were happy indeed:

> *Blessed (happy, fortunate, to be envied) is he who has forgiveness of his transgression continually exercised upon him, whose sin is covered.*
> *Blessed (happy, fortunate, to be envied) is the man to whom the Lord imputes no iniquity and in whose spirit there is no deceit.*
>
> Psalm 32:1–2

But the blood of Jesus Christ obtained something better for us. It took us **beyond forgiveness into justification. Our sins were not just covered, they were blotted out.** We are not just forgiven, we are justified. It illustrated the new covenant, of which God had spoken by the mouth of His holy prophets as a **better covenant.**

Behold, the days come, saith the LORD, that I will make a new covenant with the house of Israel, and with the house of Judah: not according to the covenant that I made with their fathers in the day that I took them by the hand to bring them out of the land of Egypt, which my covenant they brake, although I was an husband unto them, saith the LORD: But this shall be the covenant that I will make with the house of Israel; After those days, saith the LORD, I will put my law in their inward parts, and write it in their hearts; and will be their God, and they shall be my people. And they shall teach no more every man his neighbour, and every man his brother, saying, Know the LORD: for they shall all know me, from the least of them unto the greatest of them, saith the LORD: for I will forgive their iniquity, and I will remember their sin no more.

But today some people still live in the book of Leviticus. To them Christianity is all rituals, sacrifices, burnt offerings, altars and incense in the literal sense. They need to know that the blood of Jesus has settled all of that and has initiated a new and glorious way for us.

Jeremiah 31:31–34 (my emphasis)

Now, if you put your faith in the blood of Jesus Christ the Lamb of God, you are not only forgiven, but your sins are cancelled. You are purged, purified, sanctified and justified by the blood of the Lamb of God. You can now stand before God with a clean conscience, without any sense of guilt or shame. Heaven has now no record of your sins. God has declared you just, by the blood of His Son, Jesus. If this is your lot, then the line has fallen for you in pleasant places. Yes, you have a beautiful and glorious heritage (Psalm 16:6).

But the blood of Jesus Christ obtained something better for us. It took us beyond forgiveness into justification. Our sins were not just covered, they were blotted out. We are not just forgiven, we are justified.

If the saints of the Old Testament were blessed, happy and fortunate, how much more are we! We should stand firm on the blood of Jesus, rejoicing in the grace of God, never allowing the adversary to bring us into bondage again. We have received a better inheritance, a better covenant, a better standing with God than the people of the Old Testament time – only by the blood of the Lamb. What they had as a future promise we now have as a present reality.

You can see that the blood of Jesus Christ has rendered the blood of bulls and goats unnecessary for redemption. If you want to eat a goat, a lamb, a sheep or a heifer; please go right ahead. Kill the animal, shed its blood, and enjoy yourself. But to shed the blood of an animal in order to appease God, or to secure any spiritual benefit is a sheer waste of time. The blood of Jesus has secured a better and living way for us. Nothing close to it can be found by any other means.

Shed Once and for All

One other key thing that distinguishes the blood of

Jesus from the blood of the Old Testament is that it does not need to be shed again and again. It has been shed once and for all.

The blood of animals in the Old Testament time did not really satisfy the claims of God's justice. Animal blood could never fully meet the demand of his wrath (remember, in the realm of the spirit it is life for life; goat for goat; bull for bull; man for man). Animal blood could not make the people perfect. It could not take away their sin. It was only a shadow of the thing to come. The people obtained mercy and forgiveness, but were still held by the power of sin. As often as they sinned they needed fresh blood to be shed to cover that sin. The previous sacrifice was no longer effective: they had to do it again and again. This was Paul's clear argument in the book of Hebrews:

> For the law having a shadow of good things to come, and not the very image of the things, can never with those sacrifices which they offered year by year continually make the comers thereunto perfect. For then would they not have ceased to be offered? because that the worshippers once purged should have had no more conscience of sins. But in those sacrifices there is a remembrance again made of sins every year. For it is not possible that the blood of bulls and of goats should take away sins . . . And every priest standeth daily ministering and offering oftentimes the same sacrifices, which can never take away sins.
>
> Hebrews 10:1–4,11

With the blood of the animals of the Old Testament shed again and again, the people were still haunted by the bitter memory of the sins they committed, even though they had obtained forgiveness.

Then came Jesus, sent by the Father. He came in human form – a body that had been prepared for Him. While Jesus was on earth the fullness of the Godhead was dwelling in that body. He came to offer the singular sacrifice that would give the Father pleasure and deal with the problem of sin once and for all. He did it on the cross of Calvary and that sacrifice was accepted by the Father. One sacrifice for sin which was effective for ever; which fully paid the penalty and price for sin; and has the ability to cleanse, free and sustain whoever trusts in it.

> *Then said he, Lo, I come to do thy will, O God. He taketh away the first, that he may establish the second. By the which will we are sanctified through the offering of the body of Jesus Christ once for all . . . but this man, after he had offered one sacrifice for sins for ever, sat down on the right hand of God; from henceforth expecting till his enemies be made his footstool. For by one offering he hath perfected for ever them that are sanctified.*
>
> Hebrews 10:9–10,12–14

The blood of Jesus is effective in dealing with the sins of man, having accomplished the following:

- It paid the full penalty for sin, thereby meeting the full requirements of the law and fully satisfying the claims of God's righteousness.
- It can remit or blot out forever the sin of whoever trusts it. When that sin is genuinely put under the blood of Jesus in true repentance, it is blotted out forever before God.
- It can purge the conscience of whoever trusts it from the guilt, burden and shame of past sins no

matter what they were. It can purify our conscience from dead works so we can serve the
Lord effectively.

- It can sanctify whoever puts his trust in it thereby making him holy and eligible to enter into fellowship with a holy God. We are made holy by
the precious blood of Jesus Christ.
- It can deliver that individual from the sure
judgment that must come upon him or her as a
result of the sin, releasing mercy and grace
instead.
- It can cancel the power and break the grip of sin
over whoever trusts it, so you do not have to sin
again and again. Satan can no longer push you to
sin; he can only tempt. You do only what you
want to do. The power of sin is cancelled. You are
free to exercise your free-will to love the Lord
and live your life for Him.

    You cannot be held in bondage or captivity to
any sin. The blood of Jesus breaks the hold of that
sin or sinful habit forever and makes you free.
- It is ever-living, ever-flowing, ever available to
do all of the above all over again forever, as long
as it is applied in faith. It is a living blood. It
flows and it speaks for all eternity!

Jesus Christ shed His blood once and for all. It perfectly satisfied the heart of the Father and met His
holy requirements once and for all. And by that one
sacrifice for sin He has perfected for ever all who put
their trust in Him. All you need do is apply the blood
of Jesus in genuine faith and you are released from
the bondage of sin for ever. So long as you stay under
the cover of that blood, sin has no more dominion
over you. You are no longer under the law. You are

under grace – grace that is made available by the blood of Jesus, the Lamb of God. Under the cover of this blood you are forever free from the bondage of sin. Alleluia.

> For by one offering he hath perfected for ever them that are sanctified.

Hebrews 10:14

> For sin shall not have dominion over you: for ye are not under the law, but under grace.

Romans 6:14

To Be Applied by Faith

The blood of Jesus is to be applied by faith. You do not have to see it before you believe it. You do not even have to understand it before you take advantage of it. For example, each time I travel by air, all I do is just get in the plane, sit back, relax and enjoy my flight. I do not have to understand the principles of aerodynamics before I fly. But I know it works. The taste of the pudding, it has been said, is in the eating. Just step out in genuine faith in the blood of the Lamb of God and you will know it works. I never

All you need do is apply the blood of Jesus in genuine faith and you are released from the bondage of sin for ever. So long as you stay under the cover of that blood, sin has no more dominion over you.

worry myself about whether or not the plane will work; whether or not it can take off from the ground and go into the sky or whether or not it will be able to land. This is exactly what it was designed to do. This is exactly how it works.

Put your trust in the blood of the everlasting covenant and everything will be all right.

> *Present your cheque at the bank of heaven; there is no bankruptcy there! The blood of Jesus has secured it all for you.*

In Africa, I have seen people doing some funny things, saying they are applying the blood of Jesus. Some would bring coloured water in a bowl and use it to sprinkle themselves and other people, saying they are applying the blood of Jesus. Others kill a lamb or a sheep and try to use the blood on themselves and others. Some put water in a bottle. It does not work that way at all. The blood of Jesus is to be applied only by faith, for we walk by faith, not by sight. Our God is a God of faith. He wants His people to relate to Him by faith. He is pleased and honoured when we simply take Him at His Word and step out in faith.

All you need to do is as follows:

- Know that Jesus shed His precious blood for you. Believe this firmly with all of your heart.
- Find out all that the Bible says about this precious blood shed for you.

    There is power in knowledge. To be ignorant is to be vulnerable and to become a victim of superstitions and human fantasies. Genuine faith only comes by receiving the Word of God.

- Step out in faith and make your claims on the basis of what the Word of God says. If you will walk in the integrity of your heart and act in faith on the blood of the Lamb, you will find God's

Word to be true that '. . . *before they call, I will answer; and while they are yet speaking, I will hear'* (Isaiah 65:24).

It is time for you to begin to enjoy all of God's marvellous provision through the precious blood of Jesus, because it was shed for you. Step out on it today. Present your cheque at the bank of heaven; there is no bankruptcy there! The blood of Jesus has secured it all for you. Jesus has made an inexhaustible deposit for you by His precious blood. Even though it is not cheap, yet it is absolutely free. Nothing to pay. Jesus paid it all. Just present your faith cheque and it shall be honoured. The blood of Jesus has secured for you whatever you may need at the bank of heaven.

20

The Blood of the Everlasting Covenant

The LORD hath appeared of old unto me, saying,
Yea, I have loved thee with an everlasting love:
therefore with lovingkindness have I drawn thee.
Jeremiah 31:3

I was meditating on the Scriptures recently in the book of Hosea. God was complaining about Ephraim's professed love and affection for Jehovah. He said Ephraim's love for Him was like the morning mist. Transient. Unreliable. It soon vanishes into the air. God said:

O Ephraim, what shall I do unto thee? O Judah,
what shall I do unto thee? for your goodness is as a
morning cloud, and as the early dew it goeth away.
Hosea 6:4

What a contrast to God's love for us. He has loved us with an everlasting love. He has drawn us to Himself with His unfailing lovingkindness. I am glad that God has loved me with an eternal love; I can rest in His love and be assured that I am secure in time and in all eternity. Glory to His blessed name.

The basis of this everlasting love, and why it is so secure, is what we want to look into in this chapter.

When Israel (referred to as Ephraim in the above passage) failed to respond to the first covenant God made with her, He cancelled it and established the second.

> *For if that first covenant had been faultless, then should no place have been sought for the second. For finding fault with them, he saith,*
> *Behold, the days come, saith the Lord, when I will make a new covenant with the house of Israel and with the house of Judah.*

Hebrews 8:7–8

God instituted a new covenant and sealed it with the precious blood of Jesus, His only begotten Son, that it might never be broken or abrogated. This is why the blood of Jesus Christ is referred to as the blood of the New Testament or the blood of the new covenant.

> *Likewise also the cup after supper, saying, This cup is the new testament in my blood, which is shed for you.*

Luke 22:20

The old covenant was sealed with the blood of bulls and goats. But it was incapable of doing what God intended it to do. Israel, the main target of the covenant failed woefully in responding to it. They broke the terms of the covenant again and again and God had to do something new. He instituted the new covenant, based it on better promises and sealed it with the blood of Jesus.

The new covenant is far superior to the old. It is referred to as the better covenant. In all the essential points where the old covenant failed the new covenant triumphed gloriously. For example, the Old

Testament could not cancel or blot out sin. It could only secure forgiveness for those who believed; their conscience still remained under the oppressive burden of sin. But the new covenant deals with that effectively.

Actually, the Old Testament was a shadow of the New. It was to prepare God's people for the coming of Jesus, the Mediator of the new covenant. The scripture quoted at the opening of this chapter existed as a promissory note in old covenant times, awaiting fulfilment through the shedding of the blood of Jesus.

God also gave the promise in the book of Ezekiel. At the coming of our Lord Jesus, however, that which was a promise became a reality. The old covenant was the promise: the new covenant the reality, the fulfilment.

This New Testament, or new covenant, cannot be abolished or abrogated. It is everlasting. It is the fulfillment of God's original desire for Adam before the fall. It is the fulfilment of what God promised Abraham even before the law was given on Mount Sinai. It is the fulfilment of the *'sure mercy'* God gave to David. It is the fulfilment of all that the prophets prophesied in the Old Testament. It is the fulfilment of all that the patriarchs stood for and looked forward to in hope. Our Lord Jesus Christ said of Abraham: *'Abraham rejoiced to see my day: and he saw it, and was glad'* (John 8:56).

The new covenant is the actual manifestation of God's eternal love for mankind.

> *For God so loved the world, that he gave his only begotten Son, that whosoever believeth in him should not perish, but have everlasting life.*
>
> John 3:16

The new covenant, sealed with the blood of Jesus Christ, is eternal. This is why the blood of Jesus is called in the Bible **the blood of the everlasting covenant.**

> *Now the God of peace, that brought again from the dead our Lord Jesus, that great shepherd of the sheep, through the blood of the everlasting covenant, make you perfect in every good work to do his will, working in you that which is wellpleasing in his sight, through Jesus Christ; to whom be glory for ever and ever. Amen.*

Hebrews 13:20–21

Let me share with you three solid reasons why the new covenant is an eternal covenant.

Built on Love

First, it is established and built on love – the love of God for man. This love had been in the heart of the Father God before the beginning of time. It was manifested at the giving of His only begotten Son for us.

While meditating on the Scriptures the other day, I was vividly struck by this fact that God's love for man had been in His heart from the eternal past, before man was created. This is made clear in Proverbs chapter 8 where God's divine wisdom is personified. We know, according to the revelation of the New Testament,

> *The new covenant is far superior to the old. It is referred to as the better covenant. In all the essential points where the old covenant failed the new covenant triumphed gloriously.*

that Jesus is the wisdom of God:

> But of him are ye in Christ Jesus, who of God is
> made unto us wisdom, and righteousness, and sanc-
> tification, and redemption . . .
>
> I Corinthians 1:30

Now, let us read what wisdom says:

> Then I was by him, as one brought up with him:
> And I was daily his delight,
> Rejoicing always before him;
> Rejoicing in the habitable part of his earth;
> And my delights were with the sons of men.
>
> Proverbs 8:30–31

'And my delights were with the sons of men.' Think about
that.

> **The new covenant
> is the actual
> manifestation of
> God's eternal love
> for mankind.**

The first covenant was built on law. And we know the law makes nothing perfect. By the deed of the law no man shall be justified in the sight of God. But the New Testament, built on God's eternal love, remains solid and steadfast for ever.

You know the Bible says many waters cannot quench love. It is because love is eternal.

> Many waters cannot quench love,
> Neither can the floods drown it:
> If a man would give all the substance of his house for
>   love,
> It would utterly be contemned.
>
> Song of Solomon 8:7

You know that of all the three cardinal virtues the

Bible says will last for ever – faith, hope and love – the greatest of all is love.

> *And now abideth faith, hope, charity, these three; but the greatest of these is charity.*
>
> I Corinthians 13:13

You know the Bible says that God Himself is love. It does not say that God is loving, but God is love.

> *He that loveth not knoweth not God; for God is love.*
>
> I John 4:8

Love is indestructible. Love is unshakeable. Love lasts for ever. God is love and God is eternal. He has built this new covenant on the eternal, indestructible foundation of His love. The new covenant can never pass away because it is built on God.

Sealed by the Blood

When a legal document is signed and sealed, it comes into full force and cannot be violated or broken without due penalty.

When God drew up the new covenant, He sealed it with the living blood of His Son Jesus. This is awesome.

You remember the Bible says the life of the flesh is in the blood. The life of Jesus is actually flowing in His blood – the blood carries His life.

We saw how the Bible says the blood of Jesus speaks; it speaks positive things, not like the blood of of Abel. It is the living who speak. The dead do not. That the blood of Jesus speaks is an indication that it is alive; and this is what sealed the new covenant. So long as the blood is still speaking then the covenant is still in force. And, beloved, the blood speaks for ever. It can never be silent. It speaks of God's grace; God's eternal love; God's mercies that endure for ever.

The blood of Jesus Christ speaks for ever, hence, the covenant it seals is in force for ever.

> *Love is indestructible. Love is unshakeable. Love lasts for ever. God is love and God is eternal. He has built this new covenant on the eternal, indestructible foundation of His love. The new covenant can never pass away because it is built on God.*

Guaranteed by the Resurrection

The new covenant is guaranteed by the resurrection of Jesus from the dead.

The Bible makes it clear that a covenant cannot be in force until the death of the testator. You cannot execute a man's will while he is still alive, only when he dies can his written will come into effect.

We all know, though, that a man's will can be doctored and altered after his death. It is unlawful, but is sometimes done. Only those who alter the will know it has been tampered with. The dead man is no longer around to see to it that his will is done. Neither can he protest from the region of the dead.

With our Lord Jesus Christ the story is different. Having enacted the new covenant by the authority of the Father, He died, shedding His precious blood to seal the covenant and bring it into effect according to the will of the Father. But on the third day He rose from the dead, never to die again. He is alive today to see to it that His will is executed correctly, to the last word, and that His beloved ones for whom He died have what He had secured for them by His precious blood. The Bible says He lives for ever to represent us before the throne of God, interceding for us.

> *Wherefore he is able also to save them to the uttermost that come unto God by him, seeing he ever liveth to make intercession for them.*
>
> Hebrews 7:25

That Jesus actually rose from the dead and is alive today is a clear indication that the new covenant is for ever. So long as Jesus lives, the covenant is in force. And He lives for ever! He is alive for evermore.

> *I am Alpha and Omega, the beginning and the ending, saith the Lord, which is, and which was, and which is to come, the Almighty . . .*
> *I am he that liveth, and was dead; and, behold, I am alive for evermore, Amen; and have the keys of hell and of death.*
>
> Revelation 1:8,18

Secure in the Father's Love

What is the implication of all this to someone who has come to put his trust in the precious blood of Jesus? Simply, you are secure in the Father's love for ever. So long as you abide in Christ and He abides in you, nothing can shake, move or trouble you. Your relationship with the Father is secure for ever. He has loved you with an everlasting love.

This is not a matter of what you have or have not done: it is a matter of what God has done for you in Christ. There is absolutely nothing you can do to add to, or enhance the love of God for you. Now listen, you can do something to plug yourself into it. You can do something to enjoy it. You can do something to take maximum advantage of its provision. But it is there – before you knew it, while you began to understand it, after you have come into it – eternally in the heart of God, flowing towards you!

When the apostle Paul got a glimpse into the reality of God's love for us in Christ and how secure we are if we abide in His love, he proclaimed:

> *Jesus Christ is alive today to see to it that His will is executed correctly, to the last word, and that His beloved ones for whom He died have what He had secured for them by His precious blood.*

> *Nay, in all these things we are more than conquerors through him that loved us. For I am persuaded, that neither death, nor life, nor angels, nor principalities, nor powers, nor things present, nor things to come, nor height, nor depth, nor any other creature, shall be able to separate us from the love of God, which is in Christ Jesus our Lord.*

Romans 8:37–39

Be assured, beloved. Nothing can separate you from the love of God. Nothing. So long as you do not separate yourself, you are secure in the Father's love for ever. Alleluia.

This security is purchased by the blood of Jesus Christ; the blood of the everlasting covenant.

21

Bought with a Price

God told the Israelites that they were His own. They were not to worship or serve idols of any kind. There must be no strange gods among them. They were never to be servant to any man.

For unto me the children of Israel are servants; they are my servants whom I brought forth out of the land of Egypt: I am the LORD your God.

Leviticus 25:55

I was meditating on this scripture early one morning in my hotel room in Atlanta, Georgia, during a ministerial trip. At my first reading I mistakenly read verse 55 as 'bought': *'they are my servants whom I "bought" forth out of the land of Egypt.'* I began to think. God didn't want them to be slaves to anyone because he **bought** them out of slavery in Egypt. My thoughts ran wild. He paid a price for them, so He felt they were His own. In a sense, this is very true. Even though I read that scripture wrongly, I believe the Holy Spirit wanted to impress some revelation in my heart: nobody else should claim God's people as his own, they have been bought with a price. God's people are not cheap – a price has been paid for them. Each of them is precious in the sight of God. You are invaluably precious.

What price did God pay? He gave the life of every

first-born of Egypt to secure their release. The first-born of Egypt were killed by the angel of death to force the hands of stubborn Pharaoh. Obviously it pained God to do that; but it needed to be done if ever Pharaoh would let His people go. He had resisted every other move to free them before.

Often God gives other lives in the place of His own elect that are precious in His sight. Rather than have the Israelites die in slavery, shame and disgrace, He allowed some other people to die instead, that His redeemed might be free. This still happens today.

> *Since thou wast precious in my sight, thou hast been honourable, and I have loved thee: therefore will I give men for thee, and people for thy life.*
>
> Isaiah 43:4

God ordered the Israelites to kill a lamb for each household and apply its blood to make atonement for their souls. Wherever the blood was applied on the lintel of the doorpost they were covered. The angel of death would not hurt them. They were free. That was the price God paid to secure their liberty. He killed the first-born of every Egyptian and called for the blood of innocent animals.

In return for this, the children of Israel were to:

- Offer (dedicate) the first-born male to God, in lieu of the first-born of the Egyptians killed.
- Offer (sacrifice) the first-born of their animals to God in lieu of the blood of the animal that was shed.

Indeed, the redemption of their souls was precious. It cost God something. Those Egyptian males who were killed were God's precious creatures, made in His own image. Those innocent animals whose blood was shed were God's beautiful creatures. They had animal life that could not be produced in man's laboratories nor manufactured in man's factories. God had to pay for the freedom of the Israelites because of His covenant with Abraham, Isaac and Jacob.

How then were the Israelites to live their lives?

Worship Him

First, the Israelites' hearts – devotion and worship – were to be for Jehovah alone who bought them with a price. There must be no strange god among them. This God said over and over again in the Scriptures. He warned them of the stiff penalty of idol worship – to be cut off from among the people.

God's people are not cheap – a price has been paid for them. Each of them is precious in the sight of God. You are invaluably precious.

There was no sin over which God judged the Israelites of old like the sin of idolatry. He would tolerate no idols in their lives; He was jealous over them. They must be devoted to Him alone. He had brought them to Himself that they might worship Him alone with all their hearts and spirit, with all their souls, with all their might and strength.

Serve Him

Secondly, they were to serve no other but the Lord. Worship and service, though related, are different. You can serve someone and not worship him. You serve him for gain, for advantage, for benefits. But when you worship and truly adore someone you serve him devotedly, with joy and excitement; you do the most difficult job, go the extra mile and still count it a privilege.

Worship, then, is the platform for acceptable service.

God told the Israelites to serve Him alone. That did not mean they were not to work for pay or be in other people's employment. But they were not to be a slave to anyone. They were the Lord's servants as long as they walked in God's covenant.

Now back to our point. In the New Testament the price God paid to redeem us is infinitely greater than the price He paid to redeem the Israelites. Your redemption cost Him the life blood of His only begotten Son; every drop of it. He has bought you with a price. He has brought you to Himself.

For ye are bought with a price: therefore glorify God in your body, and in your spirit, which are God's.

I Corinthians 6:20

Forasmuch as ye know that ye were not redeemed with corruptible things, as silver and gold, from your vain conversation received by tradition from your fathers; but with the precious blood of Christ, as of a lamb without blemish and without spot.

I Peter 1:18–19

Hence, as He did with the Israelites of old, God is making a demand on us as His right. There is no such thing as 'something for nothing'. To receive your redemption costs you nothing, but after receiving it you are to give Him your whole life. When God takes the yoke of Satan off your neck you are to take His own yoke upon you, and be His bond-servant for ever. This is how you can find rest for your souls, for

His yoke is **easy** and His burden is **light.** In the natural sense, there is no easy yoke or a burden that is light. It is only the yoke of Jesus that is easy. It is only the burden of Jesus that is light. Only after you have taken His yoke and burden upon you can you truly be at rest.

> *Come unto me, all ye that labour and are heavy laden, and I will give you rest. Take my yoke upon you, and learn of me; for I am meek and lowly in heart: and ye shall find rest unto your souls. For my yoke is easy, and my burden is light.*
>
>   Matthew 11:28–30

His Yoke – Worship

What is His yoke? That you worship Him with all of your heart, and with all of your might, and with all of your strength. That you make Him alone your God. That you pour out your heart to Him in complete devotion; and let your eyes observe His ways.

Worship is the platform for acceptable service.

That there be no strange god or idol of any kind in your life. If you consider what He has done for you, is this too much to ask? I do not think so. As a matter of fact, He is making this demand of you because He loves you.

When you give Him your whole heart, you find life, wholeness and soundness. You find true fulfilment and complete satisfaction. You find rest and peace and joy. When you are single in your devotion to Him, He floods your entire life with His light. When you allow no idol of any kind (like sin, selfishness, lust or a habit of disobedience), then there will be no darkness of any kind in your life.

When you allow no strange god; no juju, no talisman, no foreign religion, no image, no demonic influence; no strange god at all, then you enjoy the fullness of life He offers. But the moment you allow any strange god into your life you enter into sorrow, confusion and conflict:

> *Their sorrows shall be multiplied that hasten after*
>   *another god:*
> *Their drink offerings of blood will I not offer,*
> *Nor take up their names into my lips.*
>
> Psalm 16:4

So long as Israel worshipped the Lord Jehovah alone they had no problem. He looked after them; no enemy could defeat them. He blessed them with abundance of peace, prosperity and progress; but as soon as they allowed any strange god in, they entered again into burdens of conflicts and sorrows.

In 1996 I got an insight into the reason behind the crisis in the lives of Prince Charles and Princess Diana of England. I was in the plane on my way from the United Kingdom to the United States. Just one paragraph in the newspaper said it all.

Prince Charles went to visit the largest Hindu temple in London (remember, he is the future defender of the Christian faith; a man whose ancestry gave the King James Bible to the world). According to the newspaper report, when the Prince entered the temple, the Hindu high priest met him and put a red mark on his forehead; 'the mark of faith in the Hindu god'; then the Prince **bowed** to the Hindu high priest 'as a mark of respect'. That was no **respect** at all, that was **worship.**

I had been praying for their marriage for years. I took a particular interest in it because I used their marriage in 1981 as a powerful illustration of my message.

Charles was the prince, the future king. Diana, the future queen, must be a virgin. The Bride of Christ must be pure and chaste.

Fifteen years later, both the bride and the groom had defiled and dishonoured themselves through different acts of adultery. The 'king' had entered the temple of idols to worship, and the heart of the 'queen' had been stolen by strangers. They had corrupted their ways and did not see the need for repentance. The God of heaven did not hide His wrath. It was one calamity after the other until Lady Diana died in a car crash while on a rendezvous with a Muslim boyfriend.

What does the Lord require of you as His purchased possession? Worship; complete, unalloyed, total. With all your heart, with all your being. No idol. No Hindu temple. No horoscope. No necromancy. No fortune-telling. No palm reading. No table lifting. No transcendental meditation. No juju. No enchantment. Pure, undiluted worship that flows out of genuine love and appreciation for God. Calling upon the Lord out of a pure heart. This is His yoke. Take it upon youself, beloved, and you will find it easy. Nothing else beats it. It is real.

His Burden

The second thing the Lord requests of you is your service. Your labour of love. Your complete obedience in following Him, serving Him and doing His will from the heart. Remember He has bought you with a price and He lawfully requires you to serve Him with gladness and joy, willingly and in implicit obedience. This is His burden. And His burden is light.

When God confronted Pharaoh, demanding the release of Israel from cruel bondage, He was making the demand so that Israel might serve Him. *'Let my people go,'* God said, *'that they may serve me.'* This was said to Pharaoh several times by Moses, God's servant and God delivered them that they might serve Him. He insisted they were not going to be Pharaoh's servants or anyone else's servants. They were to serve the Lord their God. If they failed to serve Him they failed in their covenant obligation and they got punished. But if they walked in obedience and served Him with all their hearts they were really blessed:

If they obey and serve him,
They shall spend their days in prosperity,
And their years in pleasures.

Job 36:11

If ye be willing and obedient, ye shall eat the good of the land.

Isaiah 1:19

This is what God requires of you today as His dear child, purchased with His precious blood. He wants you to serve Him in love. He wants you to go the extra mile as you serve in His house (the church you attend); as you get involved in evangelism and missions to rescue the perishing; as you give generously; as you intercede. All these you do to promote His Kingdom – to get souls saved, to bless and edify His saints, to minister to His faithful servants, to advance the cause of the gospel – in love and sincerity. He takes note of them in order to reward your labour of love. Your zeal and devotion to His Kingdom is sweet music in His ears. Your joyful obedience is a joy to His heart. And He rejoices to bless you because you are faithful to Him. He spares you as a man spares his son who serves him, and makes you His treasure: a jewel precious to Him. This is what He wanted to make out of Israel of old but they failed to respond to Him. This is what He wants to make out of you today. You must not fail to respond to His love.

You can choose what you want to do. You can choose whom you want to serve. You can choose to obey and serve self and sin which ends in death and destruction. Or you can choose to serve God and obey Him in righteousness and reap a harvest of abundant life here on earth, and eternal life and glory hereafter. Choose today.

> Know ye not, that to whom ye yield yourselves servants to obey, his servants ye are to whom ye obey; whether of sin unto death, or of obedience unto righteousness? But God be thanked, that ye were the servants of sin, but ye have obeyed from the heart that form of doctrine which was delivered you. Being then made free from sin, ye became the servants of righteousness.

Romans 6:16–18

Joshua, having a clear understanding of why God brought him out of Egypt, chose to worship and serve the Lord. He made his choice.

He challenged the people of his day to make their choice, to forsake all idols and serve the Lord in sincerity and truth. He made them know that it pays to serve the Lord.

Now therefore fear the LORD, *and serve him in sincerity and in truth: and put away the gods which your fathers served on the other side of the flood, and in Egypt; and serve ye the* LORD. *And if it seem evil unto you to serve the* LORD, *choose you this day whom ye will serve; whether the gods which your fathers served that were on the other side of the flood, or the gods of the Amorites, in whose land ye dwell: but as for me and my house, we will serve the* LORD.*

Joshua 24:14–15

> **You can choose what you want to do. You can choose whom you want to serve. You can choose to obey and serve self and sin which ends in death and destruction. Or you can choose to serve God and obey Him in righteousness and reap a harvest of abundant life here on earth, and eternal life and glory hereafter.**

Joshua was blessed because of his choice.

I challenge you today to choose, like Joshua of old, to **worship** and **serve** the Lord who has bought you with His precious blood. Make up your mind to worship Him worthily and to serve Him acceptably with reverence and godly fear. Lay your all on the altar for His fire to consume. Make your choice to go the extra mile for Him. Give Him your whole heart. Commit yourself to be obedient to His Word.

Worship and service – these are His yoke and burden. These are the wings on which you soar like an eagle. These are the feet on which you stand and walk with Him as a man walks with his friend.

He has bought you with a price. He shed His precious blood for you. You are no longer to live for yourself. You are to live for Him who loves you and has given Himself for you. Worship and serve Him. This is your duty. This is your obligation. This is your joy. This is your life. There is no other true fulfilment in life. Make your choice today to be obedient to His voice. You will be glad you did.

If they obey and serve him,
They shall spend their days in prosperity,
And their years in pleasures.

Job 36:11

22

You Are Precious

I will praise thee; for I am fearfully
and wonderfully made:
Marvellous are thy works;
And that my soul knoweth right well.
Psalm 139:14

You are precious! This is a message every believer needs to hear today, and not just the believer; every single human being needs to know that he has worth, he has dignity, he is precious. David understood this well, hence, he said to God, *'I will praise thee for I am fearfully and wonderfully made . . .'* (Psalm 139:14).

We have been told how bad, how evil and how terrible we are, and not without justification. Without a sense of dignity man's behaviour is unruly; without a sense of sanctity man's behaviour is evil. Lack of understanding of how precious we are in God's sight has driven many far from the love of God into the arms of the devil. Satan then oppresses them, twists their personality in a way contrary to God's original plan and purpose in order to abort the beautiful destiny they have in God, so that instead they may end up with him in the everlasting fire of hell.

But let me tell you this. You are precious. Perhaps you've been called by a teacher an empty head, a nonentity. Maybe your parents have rejected you, and labelled you a failure and a disgrace; or your husband has abused, misused and divorced you. Maybe you have been betrayed by a trusted friend. Things may have happened to you to communicate the devil's message that you are of no value. And perhaps you have believed it, giving up on yourself. Listen to this: before God Almighty, you are a jewel, a pearl of inestimable value, the apple of His eye. You are precious.

That is why when God made you, He made you in His image, after his likeness:

> *So God created man in his own image, in the image of God created he him; male and female created he them.*
>
> Genesis 1:27

He made you blessed, not cursed:

> *And God blessed them, and God said unto them, Be fruitful, and multiply, and replenish the earth, and subdue it: and have dominion over the fish of the sea, and over the fowl of the air, and over every living thing that moveth upon the earth.*
>
> Genesis 1:28

He has given you dominion over all the works of His hands.

He has given you the ability to subdue all opposition.

He has given you seed, that you may reproduce, replenish the earth. The greatest miracle on earth exists in the form of a seed. Greatness and perpetuation come only through the seed.

He has crowned you with glory and honour.

He has put all of His creation under your feet.

Read the song of love and appreciation David sang to God after he discovered his own worth in his God:

> O LORD, our Lord,
> How excellent is thy name in all the earth!
> Who hast set thy glory above the heavens.
> Out of the mouth of babes and sucklings hast thou ordained strength
> Because of thine enemies,
> That thou mightest still the enemy and the avenger.
> When I consider thy heavens, the work of thy fingers,
> The moon and the stars, which thou hast ordained;
> What is man, that thou art mindful of him?
> And the son of man, that thou visitest him?
> For thou hast made him a little lower than the angels,
> And hast crowned him with glory and honour.
> Thou madest him to have dominion over the works of thy hands;
> Thou hast put all things under his feet.
>
> Psalm 8:1–6

Beloved, make no mistake about it. The process of creation proves that, before God Almighty, you are precious.

Even when the enemy came to deceive man and man fell, Satan only succeeded in defacing the image of God in man. He could not remove or erase it altogether. Just take a look at what man, even in his fallen state has been able to accomplish and you will be convinced that we share God's image, we share God's dignity, we partake of God's ability.

After our London International Power Conference

in 1995, I took time to see off my friend from Atlanta, Pastor Creflo A. Dollar, who had come to minister with me at the meeting. He had left his own jet at an airport in New York where he had boarded the Concorde for London. I saw the Concorde, the prince of the air, sitting majestically on the tarmac in London. It took off with a roaring sound, reaching supersonic speed. Three and a half hours later, my friend was back in New York to get on his own plane. Three and a half hours from London to New York! This is what man has done.

Without a sense of dignity man's behaviour is unruly; without a sense of sanctity man's behaviour is evil. Lack of understanding of how precious we are in God's sight has driven many far from the love of God into the arms of the devil.

During one of my recent trips abroad, I could not but marvel at God's image in man. I was to fly on a Boeing 747. I saw the huge airplane getting ready for the flight. Over three hundred and fifty human beings and several tons of cargo were to be carried on board. Yet that giant of an airplane took off from the ground to a very great altitude travelling at the unbelievable speed of almost 1,000 kilometres per hour! Human ingenuity – a clear expression of the image of God.

I read in the American newspaper, *USA Today*, of the launch of an exploratory rocket going to Mars, a trip of 113 million miles. Mind boggling!

All this is what man has done even after the fall, confirming quite clearly that man indeed was made in God's image.

Yet God has redeemed you back from the fall. He paid an awesome price to secure your redemption. The redemption of your soul is precious. It cost God the blood of His only Son Jesus. You were bought with the precious blood of God's Son, Jesus Christ our Lord. This is how precious you are.

Experts have told us that to determine how precious a commodity is you need to consider among other things the following:

Rarity: How common is it? How readily available? Sand is cheap because it is common. Gold is precious and valuable because it is very rare.

Trademark: Where was it made? Who are the manufacturers? Some items sell by name and people are prepared to pay any price because the manufacturers have established a reputation and can be trusted.

The Price: What price are people prepared to pay for it? I have some shirts I bought for about $3 and I have some shirts I bought for about $30. I treat them differently. Nothing will make me pay $30 for a shirt that is only worth $3. But when I find a particular quality of shirt, I am ready to pay the price.

Now let us apply these facts. How valuable do you think you are? Let me give you a clue to the answer.

Rarity: If it were possible to bring together all the six billion people on earth today and take their fingerprints, and if you compared them with your own, you would find there is none quite like yours; not even your mother's or that of your identical twin. You are unique. There is no one like you on the surface of the earth! You are a special, unique person.

You are not a copy of anyone else. There is only one you in existence. There cannot be another you again. That is how precious you are!

Trademark: You bear the image and the identity of God. You bear the trademark of heaven. You were made in God's image and likeness. That is how precious you are!

The Price: You are so valuable and precious to God, He was ready to pay any price for you. Gold, silver, precious stones and all the money of the earth are not of enough value to purchase you. It took the life-blood of Jesus Christ, God's own Son to purchase you. That is how precious you are!

Forasmuch as ye know that ye were not redeemed with corruptible things, as silver and gold, from your vain conversation received by tradition from your fathers; but with the precious blood of Christ, as of a lamb without blemish and without spot.

I Peter 1:18–19

Now then beloved, see yourself as God sees you. You are not scum. You are not a sham. You are not a bum. You are not a dunderhead. You are not a zombie. You are not a nonentity. You are God's own image. You are the apple of His eye. You are the work of His hands.

Now then beloved, see yourself as God sees you. You are not scum. You are not a sham. You are not a bum. You are not a dunderhead. You are not a zombie. You are not a nonentity. You are God's own image. You are the apple of His eye. You are the work of His hands. You are the sheep of His pasture.

You are the sheep of His pasture.

> *Know ye that the LORD he is God:*
> *It is he that hath made us, and not we ourselves;*
> *We are his people, and the sheep of his pasture.*
> *Enter into his gates with thanksgiving,*
> *And into his courts with praise:*
> *Be thankful unto him, and bless his name.*
>
> Psalm 100:3–4

You are a child of God. You are a vital part of the body of Christ. You are part of His Bride; bone of His bones and flesh of His flesh. You have been chosen by God in Christ before the foundation of the earth. You are washed, you are justified and you are sanctified in the name of the Lord Jesus. This is who you are.

> *But ye are a chosen generation, a royal priesthood,*
> *an holy nation, a peculiar people; that ye should*
> *shew forth the praises of him who hath called you*
> *out of darkness into his marvellous light.*
>
> I Peter 2:9

Do not ever again let the devil run you down. Assume responsibility for your identity, and begin to walk and live as a prince on earth, showing forth the praise and the glory of our God.

23

Nothing But the Blood

Robert Lowry got it exactly right when he composed his hymn, 'Nothing But The Blood,' hundreds of years ago.

There can be no redemption for man outside of the blood of Jesus. As a matter of fact, if the blood of Jesus had not been shed, God would have no option but to send man to burn in hell for ever because of his sins. If the blood of Jesus had not been shed, there could be no relationship between God and man, there could be no forgiveness, there could be no cleansing: holiness would have been impossible. Consequently there would have been no chance of any man ever entering heaven because nothing unclean can enter there.

If the blood of Jesus had not been shed there would have been no deliverance from the grip of the devil, there would have been no freedom. We all would have had to live and die in bondage to the devil and all his works and be lost forever.

If the blood had not been shed, there would have been no basis for man to enjoy the blessing of God. No blessing, no favour, no covenant, without the blood of Jesus. All sins are purged by the blood; all blessings are secured by the blood. Without the blood of Jesus man will be eternally separated from God.

You may ask, what about the saints of the Old

Testament time like Abraham, Moses, David and Daniel? How did they succeed in relating to God as they did? Remember Jesus Christ is the Lamb of God *'slain from the foundation of the world'*. What God did from the foundation of the world was only manifested at Calvary. Adam and Eve looked towards it when God shed the animal blood in order to clothe them with coats of skins instead of their leaves (Genesis 3:21). Abraham looked towards it when he offered his son, Isaac. Each time Aaron presented the animal blood before the mercy seat in the holy place, he looked forward in hope to the time when Messiah would come. They were all saved in hope. That was why Moses and Elijah met with Jesus at the Mount of Transfiguration to discuss His death and resurrection because that is where their ultimate salvation lies. The saints of the Old Testament at their death could not go straight to heaven. They went to Abraham's bosom or as the Scriptures often put it were *'gathered unto their fathers'*. At the resurrection of Jesus Christ, *sheol* was opened and *'many bodies of the saints which slept arose, and came out of the graves after his resurrection, and went into the holy city, and appeared unto many'* (Matthew 27:52–53). Jesus Christ actually arose to lead them out of their captivity right to the throne of God. Their salvation

> *If the blood of Jesus had not been shed there would have been no deliverance from the grip of the devil, there would have been no freedom. We all would have had to live and die in bondage to the devil and all his works.*

hinged on the death and resurrection of our Lord Jesus Christ.

For both the Old and New Testament saints nothing else can save but the blood of Jesus.

But thank God, the blood was shed! It is available to everyone.

You do not need to bring anything to qualify for redemption. You do not need to bring anything to qualify for the blessing and the covenant. You do not need anything to qualify for heaven and for glory. Come just as you are, via the blood. Jesus' blood is sufficient. Nothing else is acceptable. Nothing but the blood of Jesus. And if you come via the blood all things are ready for you to freely and fully enjoy; freely and fully.

24

The 42nd Generation

When Jesus was on the cross something happened. To find out whether or not He had died they ripped open His side and out of the riven side blood and water flowed. From the side of our Lord a generation of the righteous was born washed by the water and the blood, made free for ever.

This is the generation which will not pass away until they see the Kingdom of God in glory and power. This is the missing 42nd generation in Matthew chapter 1. This is the seed which is going to serve Him and declare His generation on earth.

Please let me explain this.

Matthew chapter 1 begins thus:

*The book of the **generation** of Jesus Christ, the son of David, the son of Abraham . . .*

Matthew 1:1 (my emphasis)

This is how the whole of the New Testament started. It is not a book of the **genealogy** of Jesus Christ. It is a book of the **generation** of Jesus Christ. It is all about what Jesus Christ generated into the earth.

But did he have a son to carry on His name? After all He did not marry a wife or have a child. And in the prophetic lamentation for Him, it was written that there was no one to declare His generation, to carry on His lineage or to declare His name. Was that not what Isaiah said in his prophecy?

*He was taken from prison and from judgment: **and who shall declare his generation?** for he was cut off out of the land of the living: for the transgression of my people was he stricken.*

Isaiah 53:8 (my emphasis)

He did not marry. He had no child. Who shall declare his generation? This is the greatest lamentation to be made for any man who died in Israel. In those days the greatest pain was for a man not to have a son to carry on his name. And that was the case with our Lord Jesus, in the flesh. However, the entire New Testament begins as *'The book of the **generation** of Jesus Christ'*.

Now, back to Matthew chapter 1, the summary of the generations up to Jesus Christ is contained in verse 17.

So all the generations from Abraham to David are fourteen generations; and from David until the carrying away into Babylon are fourteen generations; and from the carrying away into Babylon unto Christ are fourteen generations.

Matthew 1:17

If from Abraham to David were fourteen generations, from David to the carrying away of the captives were fourteen generations and the carrying away captive until Jesus were fourteen generations then there should be forty-two generations in all.

However, if you study verses 1 to 16 closely you will discover only forty-one generations which terminated in Christ Jesus who, according to the flesh, did not produce another generation.

Where then is the 42nd generation? Let us resolve this riddle by referring to just three scriptures. Firstly:

*The book of the **generation of Jesus Christ**, the son of David, the son of Abraham.*
                    Matthew 1:1 (my emphasis)

As I mentioned, Matthew is not about the genealogy of Jesus Christ, but about the generation of Jesus Christ. This means He actually generated something into the earth, and the book of Matthew (and the entire New Testament) is about that generation.

*Yet it pleased the LORD to bruise him; he hath put him to grief: **when thou shalt make his soul an offering for sin, he shall see his seed, he shall prolong his days,** and the pleasure of the LORD shall prosper in his hand. He shall see of the travail of his soul, and shall be satisfied: by his knowledge shall my righteous servant justify many; for he shall bear their iniquities.*
                    Isaiah 53:10–11 (my emphasis)

'*When thou shalt make his soul an offering for sin, he shall see his seed, he shall prolong his days . . .*'? Wait a minute, Isaiah. You have lamented that this man, having no seed, has nobody to declare his generation (v 8). How come you turn around to say, '*he shall see his seed*'? Where does the seed come from if not from the womb of a woman; He never married, remember?

'*When thou shalt make his soul an offering for sin, he shall see his seed . . .*' The seed of Jesus actually came forth when God made His soul an offering for sin.

Just as God opened the first Adam's side and brought forth his wife Eve, God caused the side of Jesus to be opened and brought out a special generation. It is a generation which shall love and adore Him. It is a generation that shall be His bride. It is a generation which shall serve him. A people created and recreated. A people that will declare His generation and proclaim His name upon the earth. Let us look at the final clue in the redemption psalm:

A seed shall serve him;
It shall be accounted to the Lord for a generation.
They shall come, and shall declare his righteousness
Unto a people that shall be born, that he hath done
this.

Psalm 22:30–31

A seed (singular) shall serve Him.

This seed shall be accounted to the Lord for a generation. 'They' (plural; that is to say this generation) shall come, and shall declare His righteousness.

This is talking about the Church of Jesus Christ (singular) with her many-member body (plural). That was the generation that was born when Jesus hung upon the cross and shed His precious blood. This is the bride of Christ. When God wanted to give a bride to the first Adam, He put him to sleep and opened up his side and took out Eve. When Jesus the last Adam was to have a bride, a people that will declare His generation, God caused His side to be opened and out of the riven side came His bride. A people that will serve Him. We are the 42nd generation. We shall proclaim His righteousness upon the earth. We are proud to declare His generation.

That 42nd generation is still upon the earth today. Many of its members have gone to heaven but the generation is still here; the last true generation – one family, one blood. This generation shall not pass away until the Kingdom of God comes in power and in glory. We are His seed. We shall declare His glory. We shall declare His righteousness. We shall declare His generation. We are proud to be called by His name. It is all by the blood of the Lamb. Nobody can be part of this generation until he or she comes by the water and the blood.

> *We are the 42nd generation. We shall proclaim His righteousness upon the earth. We are proud to declare His generation.*

Rejoice if you are a part of this glorious generation. The lines have fallen to you in pleasant places. You have a good heritage.

If you are not yet part of this generation, this is your opportunity. The fountain of life opened at Calvary is still flowing. Through the precious blood of Jesus you can be born into the family of God today.

Glory to the Lamb!

And they sung a new song, saying, Thou art wor-
thy to take the book, and to open the seals thereof:
for thou wast slain, and hast redeemed us to God
by thy blood out of every kindred, and tongue, and
people, and nation; and hast made us unto our God
kings and priests: and we shall reign on the earth.
Revelation 5:9–10

It is not an overstatement at all to say that we owe
all we are to the redeeming blood of Jesus Christ
our Lord.

Without this blood there is no forgiveness of sins.
Even after we are saved we could still be lost if not for
the blood that cleanses us from our numerous faults
and makes us acceptable to God. Right now when
God looks at you, He does not just see a dirty, sinful
you; He sees you covered with the blood of Jesus.
That is if you have been born again, walking in the
Spirit.

None of us would be a match for the devil if we
were to be left alone. But the blood of Jesus not only
delivered us from the awful grip of Satan, but also
gave us complete victory over him. Now we can say
boldly 'I am more than a conqueror over the devil,
because Jesus shed His blood for me'.

Finally, it is by the blood of Jesus we will enter our

eternal home. We must be upright, pure, holy and true to God and His Word. We must be full of good works, thereby showing that we belong to God. We must bring forth the fruit of repentance, never going back to that filth out of which we have been delivered. We must resist the enemy and overcome every temptation as we continue in our onward journey to heaven. All of this is made possible by the blood of the Lamb. Nothing else qualifies us for victory and glory but the blood of Jesus.

This is why the saints will sing praises to the Lamb for ever and ever, because He has redeemed us by His precious blood. But before we get to the pearly gates, before the new heaven and the new earth appear, let us keep on singing His praises and glory no matter how feebly. It shall get sweeter still when, on the golden shore, we come to fully appreciate what the precious blood of Jesus has done for us.

Be grateful to God in your heart forever. The blood of Jesus was shed for you.

JESUS IS LORD.

About the Author

- Francis Wale Oke committed his life to Christ as Saviour and Lord in December 1975.
- He began to preach the gospel in December 1976.
- He stepped out into full-time ministry in obedience to the Holy Spirit in May 1982.
- He founded The Sword of The Spirit Ministries in 1983.
- He was ordained formally into the ministry in February 1986 after close to ten years of ministry labour and experience.
- He has conducted Mass Crusades all over Nigeria and around Africa with a record crowd of over 250,000 in a single service, and tens of thousands soundly born again and filled with the Holy Spirit.
- Has travelled and spoken to more than 10,000 audiences in several countries, including Britain, the USA, Poland, Portugal, Switzerland and several African nations.
- He is a noted author of over 40 books including, *Alone with God, The Weapon of our Warfare, Victory in Spiritual Warfare.*
- He hosts a daily radio broadcast on the Nigeria national station, FRCN and several other radio stations.
- He hosts a daily television broadcast on the Nigeria Television Authority and several other television stations.
- He has appeared often on TBN and other American TV stations.
- He holds an annual God's End-Time Army

Conference in Ibadan, Nigeria for ministers of the Gospel with a definite divine calling.

- He is the founder of the International Bible College of Ministries having its main campus in Ibadan, with several satellite campuses all over Nigeria.
- He is a founding Trustee of Maranatha Ministeria Fellowship International (MMFI).
- He is the editor-in-chief of *The Sword of The Spirit* and *He Is Alive* magazines.
- He is the Board Chairman of His Kingdom House Publishers.
- He has had more than 10,000 accept the call into full-time ministry under his ministry.
- Was given a honourary doctorate degree by the Oral Roberts University in conjunction with All Nations for Christ Bible Institute, Benin City in November 1991.
- He was given the 1996 Merit Award for outstanding contribution to Religious Harmony and Human Development by the Federal Radio Corporation of Nigeria.
- He is available to serve the entire Body of Christ as the Lord leads.
- Dr Francis Wale Oke is married to Victoria and they have two children, Dorcas and Isaac.

ALONE WITH GOD

FRANCIS WALE OKE

'I have found Alone With God *very helpful myself and
believe you will experience God speaking to you and
encouraging you as you read it.'*
Colin Urquhart, from his Foreword

Born from the experience and teaching of the author,
Alone With God is a vital guide to establishing a
living relationship with God in prayer.

*'There is no limit to the possibility opened up by faith and
prayer, but'* writes Francis Oke, *'only those who take
time to really pray prove this to be true. No Christian can
ever graduate from the school of prayer this side of heav-
en: the more you pray, the more you wish to pray effectively. We should all not only know how to pray, but
actually how to make prayer a vital part of our life!'*

0 946616 86 8

WEAPONS OF OUR WARFARE

FRANCES WALE OKE

It is imperative for every Christian to understand
spiritual warfare and to know the weapons God
has provided us with. This inspired, instructive,
challenging and encouraging book will help build
up the reader and show how – in the Lord –
we are more than conquerors.

God has given us armour for protection and
weapons for use in attack so that we might know
his victory against the enemy. Francis Wale Oke
outlines these weapons and defences: the belt
of truth, the breastplate of righteousness,
the shield of faith, the helmet of salvation and
the sword of the Spirit. He shows us how to go out
in victory with our feet fitted with the Gospel of
peace and in the prayer of the Spirit.

We wrestle not against flesh and blood, but against
principalities, against powers, against the rulers of the
darkness of this world, against wickedness in high places.
Ephesians 6:12

1 897913 15 X

VICTORY IN SPIRITUAL WARFARE

FRANCES WALE OKE

- Do you want victory – over sin and the devil?
- Do you know how to claim that victory?
- Are you enjoying the fruit of victory in your daily life?

In this clearly-written, challenging book, Francis Wale Oke tells you how you can apply the answers to these questions in your life – through the victory that Jesus purchased with his precious blood. *'Jesus Christ is coming,'* says the author *'for the people that are holy and pure, strong and energetic, daring and bold who are making demons submit and the world tremble.'*

Francis Wale Oke fearlessly exposes the enemies we contend with, describes the weapons at our disposal and how we can best use them so as to become 'overcomers' – those who have accepted Jesus as Lord and Saviour and claimed the wonderful promises given by him.

'It is rare to see emphasis in writing on overcoming and and the overcomers. For me this has been a stimulus to faith, holiness and continuing the race set before me. Francis' book will challenge us to win the fight and win the crown'.

Roger Forster, from his Foreword

0 86347 200 1

Other Books by Francis Wale Oke

Alone With God
Arise And Shine
Deliverance On Mount Zion
Don't Lose Your Focus
Enjoy Divine Favour
Faith For Your Miracle
God's Provision For Your Complete Healing
Go Forward
He Cares For You
Let Us Pass Over Unto the Other Side
Possess Your Possession
Prevailing Prayers
Receiving The Power Of The Holy Spirit
The Weapons of Our Warfare
The Power That Works In Us
The Precious Blood Of Jesus
Turn To The Rock and Drink
Victory In Jesus' Name
Victory In Spiritual Warfare
Walking In God's Covenant

Teaching Tapes (Audio) by Francis Wale Oke

Arise And Shine
Absolute Victory
A Change of Identity
Bringing Down The Glory
The Snare Is Broken
Turn To The Rock And Drink
Let Us Pass Over Unto The Other Side
Is Your Name Written In The Book Of Life?

The Danger of Compromise
Let The Fire Fall
Walking In God's Covenant
From Curses To Blessings
The Pursuit Of Holiness
Anointing For Wealth
Christian Dressing
Divine Intervention
3-Dimensions of Warfare
Family Life I, II, III
Overwhelming Anointing.

Teaching Tapes (Video) by Francis Wale Oke

Bringing Down The Glory
New Wine For Your Life
Victory By Your Right Hand
The Pursuit Of Holiness
Anointed With Fresh Oil
Overwhelming Anointing
From Curses To Blessings
A New Anointing
The Power To Get Wealth
Walking In God's Covenant
From Glory To Glory
The Glory Of The Latter House
The Blessings Of Abraham
Moving With The Cloud Of Glory
The Foundation For An Effective Ministry
Power In The Word
Let The Fire Fall
Family Life I, II, III
Overwhelming Anointing